So You Want to Be
a School Board Member?

So You Want to Be a School Board Member?

William Hayes

The Scarecrow Press, Inc.
Scarecrow Education
Lanham, Maryland, and London
2001

SCARECROW PRESS, INC.
SCARECROW EDUCATION

Published in the United States of America
by Scarecrow Press, Inc.
4720 Boston Way
Lanham, Maryland 20706
www.scarecrowpress.com

4 Pleydell Gardens, Folkestone
Kent CT20 2DN, England

British Library Cataloguing-in-Publication Information Available

Library of Congress Cataloging-in-Publication Data

Hayes, William, 1938–
  So you want to be a school board member? / William Hayes.
    p. cm. — (A Scarecrow education book)
  Includes bibliographical references (p.) and index.
  ISBN 0-8108-4141-X (pbk.)
  1. School board members—United States. 2. School boards—United
States. I. Title. II. Series.

LB2831 .H36 2001
379.1'531—dc21   2001041157

♾™ The paper used in this publication meets the minimum requirements
of American National Standard for Information Sciences—Permanence of
Paper for Printed Library Materials, ANSI/NISO Z39.48-1992.
Manufactured in the United States of America.

Contents

As a high school principal for four years and a superintendent for over twenty-one years, I have calculated that I have participated in over six hundred school board meetings. There were also hundreds of committee meetings, sessions with advisory groups, and large public meetings on specific issues. In thinking back on these experiences, I can remember times of laughter and occasional tears. Often the topics were trivial, but there were also sessions when important educational decisions were made.

It was at these meetings when the priorities of the district were determined and where my "marching orders" as an administrator were made clear. Decisions were made to sell or close buildings, to build new ones, to initiate programs, or to terminate them. My memories of these times are, for the most part, positive. As a superintendent, I was fortunate to work with board members who sincerely wanted to have a good school system and who almost always worked together for positive ends. Some errors of judgment were made. Too often they occurred because I had not provided the necessary information upon which to base a proper decision.

It is now clear to me that some board members made personal sacrifices during their terms of office. Even though they gave generously of their time and energy, they were unfairly criticized on a number of occasions by school employees, as well as their fellow citizens. With few exceptions, there was no one who thanked them for their hard work. Still, I believe they would be unanimous in the feeling that being a member of a school board was a meaningful and rewarding way to serve their community. That is not to say that some school board members did not become frustrated and discouraged. Nearly all of them were surprised by the limitations on their power as board members. State and federal laws that govern so many aspects of school life often seemed to them to be overly burdensome. Even though board members sometimes feel hindered in bringing about desired change, they cannot help but be aware that there are also hard and important decisions to be made at the local level. Even at a time when it would seem that the influence of local boards is declining, there remain many decisions that need to be made by representatives of the local community. Officials in Washington, D.C., or the state capital cannot effectively determine an acceptable property tax rate for a community, what interscholastic sports should be offered in a school district, or who should serve as superintendent of schools. Bus routes, discipline policies, and the maintenance of buildings and grounds are examples of other issues that are best determined at the local level.

Because of tasks such as these, it becomes essential that active and interested citizens be willing to come forth to serve as board of education members. In recent years, some communities have had difficulty finding qualified candidates. In a number of school districts, individuals have sought board membership because they had a particular concern. This might be the result of a desire to lower taxes or an attempt to dismiss a superintendent or other administrator. Instead of a broad concern for the welfare of the children of the district, their objectives were narrowly focused. Some of these single-issue candidates eventually became effective board members as they learned to function as part of a team, but others have caused major disruptions in the functioning of the board of education.

The purpose of this book is to inform potential candidates about the role of school boards in our society and to offer some specific advice on how to become an effective board member. Special emphasis is given to the major issues boards are likely to face during the next decade. It is not my goal to give "the answer" to these difficult dilemmas, but rather to offer the arguments that surround the questions.

In addition, the primary task of boards of education will be examined in detail. Choosing a superintendent, passing a budget or bond issue, and dealing with the local media will be discussed. Readers will also be asked to think about ethical problems that inevitably face individual board members. The impact on one's family life is also an important consideration when an individual considers becoming a candidate.

Practical matters such as the election process are also discussed. Preparing for meetings and doing one's homework is emphasized as being vital to performing the job of a board member. Technical issues such as finance and school law must also be understood if a board member is to make good decisions on many of the complex problems that will be faced. In addition, the all-important task of choosing a superintendent is given special attention.

Once the chief school officer is selected, board members must develop an effective working relationship. Every district must find the appropriate division of responsibility between the administration and the board. Conflict between school boards and their administrations, as well as other employee groups, is an ever-present danger. The possibility of a board attempting to micromanage a district is great, but so is the equally dangerous role of becoming a mere "rubber stamp" for the policies of an aggressive superintendent. The goal must always be to develop a team approach that coordinates the work of all the parties who have an interest in the school program. Creating such a unified approach to governing and managing our schools is not a simple task, but if a board can create a cooperative environment, the potential for creating excellent schools is greatly enhanced. There are many wonderful schools in every state and to a great extent they are succeeding because of the participation of a group of talented and committed people who serve on their local school board.

My hope in writing this book is to provide potential school board candidates the information necessary to allow them to make an informed decision on whether or not to seek the position. There has never been a greater need for people who have a sincere desire to work together with others to bring about the best possible schools for our children.

Acknowledgments

I am greatly indebted to Dawn Zegers, a sophomore teacher-education major, who worked hard to type and prepare this entire manuscript. Dawn has been a true partner in this project. As with my other books published by Scarecrow Press, my wife, Nancy, proofread and made valuable suggestions that greatly improved the text. Both Dawn and Nancy played crucial roles in making this project possible.

CHAPTER 1

The Role of the Board of Education

Local citizens have been instrumental in managing our schools since the first Europeans settled in what was to become the United States. In colonial Massachusetts, a law passed in 1647 gave the people the power to establish schools. "This was the origin of the local school board."[1] Later in the seventeenth century, elected "selectmen" were given power to supervise teachers and levy taxes.[2] The idea of separate school districts also began in Massachusetts in 1789 with the passage of a law giving towns the right to "establish boundaries for school support and attendance."[3] Similar local boards were established in other states and groups of local citizens managed most schools during the eighteenth and nineteenth centuries. The powers of these appointed or elected boards included hiring and supervising teachers, raising money, and often building and maintaining school buildings. The actual official duties of local boards have continually changed during our nation's history.

Even when the Constitution and later the Tenth Amendment of the Bill of Rights seemed to make it clear that education was a power reserved for state governments, individual schools and school districts remained independent to a large degree. In the words of David Tyack in an article entitled "Democracy in Education—Who Needs It?":

> Under . . . local control, school trustees constituted the most numerous class of public officials in the world; in some states, there were as many as 45,000 local school trustees, often outnumbering teachers. Decentralized governance addressed public distrust of government by putting the school and its trustees everywhere under the eye and thumb of the citizens. This provided democracy in education, meaning self-rule by

elected representatives of the people. Communities were able to retain collective decisions about schooling—who would teach, how much schools would cost, and what kind of instruction to offer. If district voters disagreed with school trustees, they could elect others.[4]

The development of the "common school" during the second quarter of the nineteenth century saw an increase in the authority of state governments, but considerable local control remained in most states. As the century came to an end, a new elite was emerging in our school districts. School administrators were hired to bring "scientific management" to our school systems.[5] Superintendents of schools and principals gradually assumed many functions previously belonging to the boards of education. As the twentieth century continued, it became common to think of the educational administrators as those charged with managing the district while school boards created policies for the administrative staff to implement.

Another trend that evolved during the first decades of the twentieth century was to keep schools out of politics. This was especially true in large cities. One of the results of these efforts was to create smaller school boards that were to be nonpartisan. Candidates would all run as independents, rather than as a candidate of a political party.

Between 1901 and 1917, White middle-class progressives urged upstanding professionals and businessmen to seek election to school boards to replace those who might have been political party regulars. These reformers believed that it was the responsibility of the leaders of the community to be active in school affairs. Prosperous and busy citizens began serving in what they perceived to be an important way to make a contribution to their communities. They frequently were quite willing to allow the professional administrators increased latitude in managing the schools.

There are some indications that board membership by the "community elite" is declining. In the past, many companies urged their management people to seek leadership positions in their community. Increased economic pressure and management downsizing now causes many citizens to spend more hours on the job and less time serving their communities. Other prominent community leaders have avoided service on school boards in some school districts because of the increasing conflict that often characterizes the issues facing boards of education.

Many problems that have put school boards on the front pages of their local newspaper involve disputes with district employees. As teachers and other school employee groups have become unionized and now engage in collective bargaining, the likelihood of conflict has increased. Such issues, along with constant wrangling over property tax rates, have caused many to avoid seeking membership on their local school board. Some others have the perception that the federal and state governments are really running our schools and that school boards have little or no real power.

It is certainly true that public education is a shared responsibility of the local, state, and federal governments. Federalism is a reality in the field of education. Because the Constitution does not specifically delegate the power to regulate education to the federal government, it has long been assumed that governing our public schools is a power reserved for state governments. At the same time, our history of local control, which predates the Constitution, has continued to maintain many important functions for the local school boards. The only exception is the state of Hawaii, which has formed a unitary, state-operated structure.[6]

Both state and federal involvement in the management of public schools is growing. State governments are pushing the academic standards movement and its companion strategy, high-stakes examinations. Many advocates of local autonomy see these initiatives as eroding the role of local school boards in determining curriculum and local academic policies. At the same time, federal Supreme Court cases involving such issues as racial segregation and church and state have greatly affected decision making at the local level. Even though Washington provides, on average, only about 7 percent of the funds used to finance public education, laws passed by Congress (including those that deal with special education and remedial education) have had a dramatic impact on local school programs and budgets.

With education being listed as the number one concern of the American public, educational governance of schools has become a major political issue. In recent years, the Republican Party has supported programs such as school choice, charter schools, and block grants rather than specific federal programs. It has been the goal of Republicans to shrink the federal education bureaucracy and to increase local control over schools. As the new century begins, the party is moving towards supporting some federal programs to improve public education. These would include such things as early literacy and national testing. Unlike the Democratic Party, they would support tax credits for private school tuition.[7]

The Democrats, on the other hand, are in favor of a more "aggressive" federal intervention in education, coupled with a hefty influx of new money for construction, expanded preschool programs, and pay raises for teachers.[8] During the 2000 presidential campaign, the party supported a ten-year, $115 billion appropriation to establish an Education Reform Trust Fund. This money was to be used to recruit new teachers, forgive federal education loans to teacher candidates, and offer $100,000 in college aid to students who agreed to teach after earning a college diploma. The plan also included money for salary increases for selected teachers and bonuses for "outstanding master teachers."[9]

It would seem that Democrats are much more willing to support major increases in federal spending for programs in the field of education. Their conservative critics argue that such initiatives will also mean a loss of local control. Liberal Democrats are likely to respond by pointing out that local control has been dependent in the past on local property taxes and this has resulted in a system that is plagued by unequal educational opportunity. They point out that as long as schools are receiving a significant portion of their funding from local property taxes, property-poor districts will never be able to provide high-quality schools. This is especially true today in our cities and in many rural areas. For those who seek additional federal intervention, it is clear that state governments have been unable or unwilling to create parity between affluent and poor districts. For many liberals, the only answer is massive federal intervention. Just as it has taken the federal government to create equal rights for minorities and women, it is felt by many that Washington must take the lead in providing equal educational opportunity for our nation's children.

Conservatives answer by saying that the federal government is not the best way to solve the problems of our schools. For them, the solution is local control and school choice. Even with these significant differences, it is unlikely that there will be dramatic changes in the way schools are managed. There will continue to be involvement by all levels of government.

Another area that has led to "the decline of school board power is teacher collective bargaining, which often determines such matters as teacher compensation, working conditions, and even curriculum questions."[10] Numerous state laws make it mandatory for school districts to negotiate with their employees all terms and conditions of employment. This includes salaries and fringe benefits, as well as hours of work. In the past, salaries and working conditions were often determined unilaterally by the administration and board of education.

A more recent trend that has affected school boards is "site-based management." The concept is that school districts will be better managed if individual schools are given the power to make some management decisions. In a number of states, school-level committees made up of the principal, teachers, parents, and sometimes high school students have been mandated. These committees have become involved in developing recommendations on discipline policies, budgets, curriculum, and even, in some cases, the hiring process. Such groups have provided additional "grassroots" input but they also sometimes complicate the decision-making process. Although most of their decisions are merely recommendations to the board, conflict can emerge when their proposals are not accepted.

With federal and state governments assuming new powers, and with employee unions and advisory groups sharing in what were once considered the sole prerogatives of the board of education, one would be tempted to conclude that school boards no longer play a major role in managing our schools. Such a conclusion would be unfortunate and inaccurate, as boards of education do remain a potent force within our school districts. What exactly are the current functions performed by school boards as we enter the twenty-first century? The answer to this question will vary somewhat from state to state, but there are many important similarities.

First and foremost, the board of education must take the leadership in developing a vision for the community's schools. This vision or mission should reflect a consensus "as to what students need in order to achieve their highest potential."[11] Once this vision is articulated, the board should adopt specific short- and long-range objectives for the district. "All board decisions should follow logically from these delineated goals and objectives."[12]

A second major function of school boards is to maintain an effective and efficient governing structure for the school district and to ensure that those who are responsible are held accountable to the community. In maintaining and developing this structure, the board has a number of important specific functions.

1. *Selecting and Evaluating the Superintendent*

   One of the most important duties of any board of education is choosing the person who will act as the chief school officer. Although many boards involve community members, faculty, staff, and sometimes students in the process, the ultimate choice belongs to the board. Because in most states a superintendent is given a contract, the board must also determine salary, fringe benefits, and other contract considerations. It is important also that the board have in place a procedure for annual evaluations of the superintendent. Increasingly, this process is tied to the superintendent's success in meeting the objectives established by the district. Ultimately, the board of education will determine whether their chief school officer will be given a contract renewal or be terminated.

2. *Creating Evaluating Policies*

   Another primary role of board members is to develop, evaluate, and monitor school policies. These policies are the rules under which the school district will function and they cover every phase of the program. There will be policies related to textbook adoption, student transportation, and school building maintenance. These and many other policies should be included in the district policy manual. If you find upon taking office as a new school board member that no such manual exists, you should suggest that one be created. Like any legislative body, boards of education are continually adding to and amending their policies. Not only is it the board's responsibility to create these rules, it is important that all policies be regularly reevaluated and their enforcement monitored.

3. *Monitoring Student Learning*

   This duty requires that the administration frequently report to the board the results of various academic assessments used by the district. If these reports appear to show that there are problems, board members must ask the hard questions and seek solutions to weaknesses in the district's program. Everyone involved in schools must constantly remember that the primary goal is student learning. Education is a dynamic field in which there will always be new curriculums and teaching methods introduced. Board members should be prepared to ask questions about these innovations and require that evidence be presented that the proposals will indeed help children to learn better. Too often, boards have been sold on new programs and have expended large amounts of money only to find out after several years that the innovations have made little difference in what students learn.

4. *Responsibility for Monitoring the Collective Bargaining Process* — Although board members probably will not be sitting at the negotiating table during contract talks with employee groups, the board must be actively involved in the process. Prior to beginning negotiations, boards of education should give to their negotiating team parameters and guidelines. These instructions need to deal not only with financial considerations but also include guidelines on shared decision making with the employee group. Is your board willing to include class size restrictions in a contract with teachers? Are you going to allow employee groups the right to approve the school calendar? Because many of these issues have historically been determined solely by the board, it is important to decide what decisions will be shared. The collective bargaining process can be one of the most disturbing and stressful aspects of board membership. Because employees often see the board as the "enemy" in collective bargaining, it is always possible that board members could find union pickets in front of their homes. They also can become targets of letter-writing attacks in the local newspaper. Despite the pressures during a period of difficult collective bargaining, board members must always remember that they are elected representatives of the community and the guardians of each child's educational opportunity.

5. *Preparing, Adopting, and Monitoring the District Budget* With the help of the school administration, the board must prepare and administer the school budget. In many districts, schools are the largest employer and have the biggest budget. The process

of developing a spending plan for the district is a complex one that includes participation by many people, but ultimately the responsibility of adopting a budget belongs to the board of education. After the budget is put in place, board members should demand regular, detailed reports. Potential overexpenditures must be identified and analyzed. Transfers of funds from one budget line to another will occur. The board should approve large transfers and cost overruns will need to be explained to the board. A district that runs out of money prior to the end of a school year will be held accountable by both their auditing firm and the citizens of the community.

The five tasks listed above are all extremely important, but the responsibilities of a board of education include more than maintaining a sound structure for the school district. A third major role is to provide community leadership. The importance of this function was articulated in a California School Boards Association publication.

As the only locally elected officials chosen to represent the interests of school children, board members have a responsibility to speak out on behalf of the children in their community. Boards are advocates for their students, their districts' educational programs and public education. They build support within their communities and at the state and national levels.[13]

While listing this important responsibility, a board must follow certain guidelines. The New York State School Boards Association suggests the following:

1. Boards must exercise their duties in compliance with state and federal law.
2. Members of Boards of Education must act as a unit rather than as individual board members.
3. Members of Boards of Education must maintain strong ethical standards and avoid conflicts of interest in performing their duties.
4. A Board of Education must develop clear rules for their meetings, included should be provision for prepublished agendas, complete minutes that are made available to all citizens, and provisions for public participation in the work of the board.[14]

To be a successful board member, one must do mo
few rules. A helpful description of successful board membc...
cluded in a publication of the California School Boards Association.
The author of that publication lists the following characteristics of successful board members:

They work well as members of a team.

- They understand that the board, rather than individuals on the
  board, establishes the policies and makes the decisions that provide direction for the school district.
- They collaborate with staff, families, other agencies, and businesses to build schools that encourage the best from all students.
- They work to improve schools by taking the time to build public
  understanding, support, and participation.

They focus their efforts on serving all children.

- They make sure every deliberation, decision, or action of the board
  takes into consideration the best interests of all the students they
  serve.
- They understand board members are entrusted by all the parents
  in the community and that no child is more important than another.

They realize demeanor has consequences and act accordingly.

- They understand that the way board members act as individuals
  and as a body affects the climate of the school district.
- They are respectful, listening carefully to colleagues, staff, parents, and the public.
- They have integrity and display professionalism, setting a tone for
  the schools that communicates the importance and seriousness of
  their work.
- They operate with fairness and sustained effort so that long-term
  changes can be implemented.
- They focus on student achievement no matter what issues arise.

They respect the diversity of perspectives and styles on the board and in the community.

- They know their board is as diverse as the community it serves.
- They respect their fellow board members' right to hold differing views.[15]

One should not be overwhelmed by the model board member described above. Instead, future board members should consider these as appropriate goals.

Finally, as we conclude this consideration of the roles of the board of education, two factors must be understood.

1. The actual roles and powers of boards of education have changed dramatically during the past three centuries and they will undoubtedly continue to be in a state of flux. Although it would appear that in recent years the powers of boards of education have lessened, they remain an important player in educational governance in this country.
2. Despite the fact that we are likely to see new initiatives in education by both state and federal governments, there remains a very powerful commitment to local control of schools. No prominent leader has even suggested that school boards should not continue to play a prominent role in managing our schools.

With these factors in mind, a person seeking membership on a local board should not hesitate because of the perception that school board members cannot make a positive difference in their communities. It would now be appropriate to consider the question of how a person can gain a position on their local board.

NOTES

1. William Drake, *The American School in Transition* (New York: Prentice Hall, 1955), 71.
2. Drake, *The American School in Transition*, 71.

3. Joel Spring, *The American School* (White Plains, N.Y.: Longmans, 1990), 141.

4. David Tyack, "Democracy in Education—Who Needs It?" *Education Week*, 17 November 1999, www.edweek.org/ew/ewstory.cfm?slug=12TYACK. h19&keywords=David%20tyack (21 September 2000).

5. Spring, *The American School*, 221.

6. Ann Bowman and Richard Kearney, *State and Local Government* (Boston, Mass.: Houghton Mifflin, 1993), 431.

7. "Bush, Gore Offer Vastly Different Education Plans," *School Board News*, 30 May 2000, www.nsba.org/sbn/00-may/053000-1.htm (10 August 2000).

8. *School Board News*.

9. *School Board News*.

10. Bowman and Kearney, *State and Local Government*, 440.

11. "School Board Leadership: The Role and Function of California's School Boards," *California School Boards Association*, www.csba.org/communications/leadership/lead.htm (21 September 2000).

12. "What Does a School Board Member Do?" *New York State School Boards Association*, www.nyssba.org/bdsupport/todolist.htm (8 September 2000).

13. *California School Boards Association*.

14. "Essential Roles and Responsibilities," *New York State School Boards Association*, www.nyssba.org/bdsupport/essential.htm (8 September 2000).

15. *California School Boards Association*.

CHAPTER 2

Becoming a Board Member

Communities use several possible methods to choose members of the board of education. One can be appointed or elected to the position. In some very few cases, a local board can have some of its members who are elected and others who are appointed. In a summary published by the Virginia School Boards Association Newsletter, one hundred communities elected their board members, thirty-five were appointed, and two had both elected and appointed members.[1]

Boards differ in other ways. The length of the term of office can vary from a two-year term to a five-year term. Some districts have adopted term limits for their members, although the vast majority of school districts do not restrict the number of terms a member can serve. Several states allow board members to be paid, but such is not the case in most school districts. Payment for service on school boards is restricted most often to urban districts. On the other hand, board members are almost always compensated for their expenses for attendance at school-related conferences or training sessions. A board member might have to pay out-of-pocket expenses for their mileage to and from regular meetings or attending school-related events, such as retirement parties. Potentially, the greatest expense might be your campaign to be elected.

In districts that elect their board members, campaigning takes place in a number of ways. Before anyone plans for campaign advertisements or signs, however, there are several questions that must be answered. First, you (the potential school board member) must determine whether the seat on the board you are seeking will be elected by all of the voters in the district or if you will be selected only by the voters in a specific geographic district. Some boards have both at-large seats as well as seats that represent merely a portion of the school district. You also need to be familiar with the term of office. In nearly all cases, board of education members have staggered terms of offices. On a nine-member board with a three-year term of office, one third of the seats would be up for election each year. Another important consideration is whether a political party controls the nomination for a place on the ballot. If the names of the political party appear on the ballot in school board elections, it is extremely helpful to receive the nomination of a major party. This is especially true if school board elections take place at the same time as the general election. Almost all school district elections are now nonpartisan. Even in our major cities, most races are independent of any party affiliation.

Prior to beginning a campaign for election to a school board, potential board members must ensure that they are legally eligible to be a candidate. Each state has established its own requirements, although those requirements tend to be almost identical from state to state. A typical list of requirements would be those outlined in California state law. You may be elected or appointed to a school board if you are:

- eighteen years of age or older
- a citizen of the state
- a resident of the school district
- a registered voter, and
- not disqualified by the constitution or laws of the state from holding a civil office.[2]

Once a person has determined eligibility, it is important to learn about any laws governing school board elections. The typical election law requires candidates to circulate petitions, which are normally available at the school district office. There is always a prescribed period prior to the election when they can be circulated and a closing date after which petitions cannot be submitted. A petition that is accepted by the school district will ensure that the candidate's name is placed on the ballot. Rules usually require a minimum number of signatures from registered voters in the district. It is always wise to significantly exceed the minimum number of signatures, as it is possible that some of the people who signed the petition are ineligible under the law. The number of required signatures varies greatly from district to district. In New York State, the law reads that "the petition must be signed by at least twenty-five qualified district voters or two percent of the number of those who voted in the previous annual election, whichever number is greater. In small city school districts, nominating petitions must be signed by at least 100 qualified voters."[3] In many districts, "write-in" candidates are allowed but the mechanics of waging a "write-in" campaign make it quite difficult.

Circulating the petition represents the beginning of a candidate's campaign. Of course you can have friends or family members circulate the petitions, but many candidates have seen this exercise as a way to meet and communicate with potential voters. Among those who should be considered for signatures would be your friends, neighbors, and relatives. It is important that these individuals know that you are a candidate. Remember that in most school district elections, the turnout can be extremely low. Often it is no more than 5 to 10 percent of the eligible voters. A solid core of friends and family can make a difference. Going door-to-door is the most common way to gather signatures, but some candidates like to take advantage of events where large numbers of people are gathered. This is an acceptable practice at some school functions, but one would not want to bother a parent for a signature during an important play at a high school football game, or when the marching band is passing by during the Fourth of July parade. In gathering signatures, you should remember all of the potential voters. This includes not only parents but also senior citizens and eighteen and nineteen year olds.

Unlike our presidential elections, the actual campaign for school board will be relatively short. Because of this, it is necessary that you have a plan in place. Before decisions can be made on your strategy, it can be helpful to know the profile of the people who are likely to vote. Voters who are primarily concerned with children and creating excellent schools are present in every district. Parents with children enrolled in the public schools are voters who have the most at stake in school elections. Many in this group are often too busy to vote unless there is a concerted effort to encourage them to come to the polls. Every district also has a group of citizens of every age who are strongly committed to education as a way to improve society. They often are citizens who are fortunate enough not to be financially threatened by tax increases. Others who are less affluent are willing to sacrifice to provide better schools for the community. During a campaign, these voters want to know what your thoughts are for improving schools. They will be supportive of a rich variety of academic programs, including music, art, special opportunities for gifted students, and advanced placement courses. This group is looking for candidates who have creative ideas and will be supportive of quality programs, even if these offerings will require higher taxes.

On the other hand, there will be citizens who also want good schools but are primarily concerned about taxes. This group can include businesspersons or farmers who feel economically pinched by increased property taxes. Others in this category would be those on fixed incomes. This is especially true of a growing number of senior citizens, who represent a significant percentage of those who vote in many districts. Some of these individuals are attempting to live almost solely on Social Security payments and the possibility of increased property taxes could theoretically result in forcing them to sell their homes. Every community also has a number of fiscally conservative individuals who resent what they consider to be excessively high teacher and administrative salaries ("they only work 180 days"). Many in this group oppose what they consider to be "frills" in the educational system. Such individuals are angered by expenditures for "all-weather running tracks," weight rooms, and acres of parking lots for student cars. Another group that can be upset by ever-increasing property taxes are those parents who are paying tuition for their children to attend private schools. Some of these parents are unhappy about paying for services they are not using. The growing number of home-school parents can also be sensitive to increases in taxes.

Those voters whose primary concern is the effect of new taxes are seeking board candidates who share their concerns about the high cost and possible inefficiency of our public schools. Many of these people believe that there are too many administrators and other nonclassroom personnel. As a candidate planning a campaign, you need to be aware that the two groups of voters described above are the most likely to turn out on election day.

Communities can be divided in another way. In every school district, there are varying degrees of trust in school officials. Those who are happy with the school district are likely to be good listeners as a candidate explains his or her ideas. They are going to take seriously any proposed plans to improve the school district. There will also be citizens who do not trust either the board of education or the administration. These individuals are likely to be skeptical about any statement made by a candidate during the campaign. Even if they agree with what the candidate says, they could very likely believe it would be impossible for any individual board member to "beat the system." These voters see politics generally as being dominated by self-seeking officeholders and administrators. Others will be quite indifferent to any election. If voter turnout is any indication, the number of cynical and indifferent voters is growing.

Knowing that you have these kinds of divisions within any community, it becomes a major challenge to plan a well-balanced election campaign. Before developing a strategy, it is important to examine your reasons for becoming a candidate. If your primary motivation is anything but seeking to help the children in your community, you might question your motives carefully. The factors that cause people to take any action in life are usually not simple, and there are bound to be mixed motives for seeking any office. It is possible that you see the school board as a "stepping stone" to higher office. That in itself is not wrong, unless it is your only motive. Assuming that you are at least in part motivated by the desire to help create a better school district and a stronger community, you need to analyze what needs to be done to accomplish these objectives. In doing so, it is helpful to ask yourself the following questions:

1. What do I believe are the current academic strengths and weaknesses of the district?
2. What, if anything, can I suggest that might improve the weak areas that have been identified?
3. Does it seem to me that district funds are being effectively managed?
4. What, if anything, can I suggest to strengthen the management of the district?
5. Is it my impression that the students and the staff are happy with the schools?
6. If there are problems with the morale of students and employees, what can I suggest to help the situation?

7. Is the current school board doing a good job?
8. What, if any, special skills and experiences can I bring to the board that might make it more effective?

The answers to these questions can help a board candidate develop some themes for the campaign. If you as a candidate have only limited knowledge of what is happening in the school district, your campaign might stress the skills and experience that you can bring to the board. Conducting a campaign based solely on your résumé will probably not be enough. You should try to reach some conclusions about some basic questions that people are likely to ask. For instance, citizens will want to know what you feel about the current tax rate. You are likely to be asked privately about your attitude toward the school administration. Voters will inquire about your position on programs for the gifted and talented and for students with special education needs. Some of the questions will be highly specific. If a candidate has not had the time to carefully study a controversial issue, it is better not to give a constituent a definitive answer that will later be a source of regret.

As you decide why it is you are running and what you hope to accomplish, you will have to determine how much campaigning you want to do and how you will pay for the campaign. Posters, brochures, mailings, newspaper ads, and signs can be quite expensive. Are you willing to spend your own money or will you ask others to contribute to your campaign? Will you accept contributions from interest groups within the community? What if the teachers' union is willing to contribute to your campaign? Companies that do business with the school district will often donate to candidates whom they believe will support their interests. These potential donors could be the company that provides student transportation for the district, the accounting firm that audits the schools' books, or the insurance broker who is seeking to represent the school district. Although in most districts there is little or perhaps no money spent during board elections, there are times when such races involve large sums. The October 10, 2000, issue of the *San Diego Union-Tribune* carried the following headline, "$500,000 Ad Campaign Targets Trustee Zimmerman." The article discusses a group of San Diego businesspersons who defeated the reelection bid of Fran Zimmerman, a vocal critic of the superintendent's "Back to Basics" program. The embattled incumbent raised nearly $26,000 from about 600 individuals to pay for her campaign.[4] This was undoubtedly an unusual race, but especially in larger districts, significant amounts of money are sometimes spent.

Before taking money from anyone, you need to know the state laws governing contributions to school board candidates. In many states, a mandated reporting procedure allows the public to know the names of your contributors. The financial assistance or formal endorsement of certain groups can actually be harmful to your campaign. In a community with a history of difficult labor negotiations, accepting money or an endorsement from a school district union can cause some voters to see you as a "tool of the union" who will "give away the store" during labor negotiations. It is equally true that if you are endorsed by or take money from a local taxpayers group, you could be seen as a candidate who cares only about lowering taxes.

Whatever your decision on campaigning contributions, it is important to keep careful records of expenditures and only use the money for legitimate campaign purposes. It is also advisable to avoid making any promises in exchange for contributions. As you consider how to spend whatever campaign budget you have, it will be necessary to make choices.

In many communities, putting up a few signs on the lawns of your friends and supporters will help people to remember your name. The signs, like any other campaign strategy, can include something more than your name. It is helpful to have a message. Are you the candidate who is going to bring your extensive business background to the local board or perhaps the person whose work in education outside the district will help you to contribute to the academic program? Perhaps you are a mother of three children and a past PTA president who has learned about school programs and wishes to now use these experiences to contribute to the board of education.

Other than the use of signs, you need to consider other campaign tactics. Of course, the least expensive is embarking on a door-to-door campaign. If you decide to do so, it is helpful to distribute a printed pamphlet or handout. These publications can also be handed out at public events. General mailings or targeted mailings, although expensive, can also be considered. If you are a candidate whose ideas will have great appeal to the senior citizens in the district, you might try to procure mailing lists from the senior citizen center. This would allow you to target a specific portion of the voting population. There are ways to obtain mailing lists of parents and other special groups as well.

It is also possible to take out ads in the local newspapers. A less expensive option is to use the penny-savers and weekly newspapers within the school district. In some more visible campaigns, radio and even television ads are used. Before spending the money on any media ads, it is important to determine whether these ads are likely to be seen by a significant number of potential voters in the district.

Along with these common types of campaigning, community groups will frequently sponsor a "Meet the Candidates Night." Less often, candidates might be asked to speak to a local church group or civic organization. Although at times the audiences at these meetings are small, they often can affect a campaign. This is especially true in a small district. A candidate making even one remark that is critical of teachers can lose many votes. Undoubtedly, word about such a comment will circulate quickly the next day in faculty rooms across the district. Likewise, a candidate who appears to be uninformed or belligerent in a public appearance can expect others to hear about it. This will occur even if the local press does not cover the event.

Although the number of local public appearances of school board candidates will be minimal in most communities, it is important to be prepared with a carefully crafted statement outlining your qualifications and the general themes of your campaign. Perhaps the most dangerous portion of these meetings for candidates is the question-and-answer period. It is essential to be gracious to both opponents and to those asking questions. At the same time, you cannot allow yourself to be drawn into discussing a subject about which you have little or no knowledge. If you have not carefully studied a controversial issue, it is probably best to avoid a definitive answer. At the same time, the audience needs to be convinced that you will fairly evaluate the issues. If they feel that you are a person who will analyze the facts and make a just decision, most people will accept your unwillingness to be specific in your answer.

Along with public appearances, the telephone can be used to help reach voters. You obviously do not want to bother people during the dinner hours. Calls to potential voters between 7:30 and 9:00 in the evening certainly can be used. Prior to doing so, it would be wise to become aware of any laws in your state regarding telemarketing restrictions. At some point within twenty-four hours before the election, it is good to have your friends and family called to remind them to be sure to vote.

During the campaign, a candidate should be as visible as possible in the community. This is especially true at school events, including concerts, PTA meetings, and athletic events. One should also try to attend all public board of education meetings. This will demonstrate a candidate's sincere interest in what is going on in the school district. Merely talking to individual voters, either by going door-to-door, at the local coffee shop, or in any public place, is perhaps the best way to campaign.

As mentioned earlier, there are a minority of districts where board members are not elected but are appointed. For those seeking to be considered for such an appointment, it is important first to find how the appointments are made. Various methods are used, but in most cases, it is a legislative body or a special committee that makes the selection. It could be the county board of supervisors, the city council, or a school board selection committee. Preparing a formal letter that expresses your interest in being considered as a candidate should be sent to the appropriate appointing body. Also included in such a mailing should be a résumé and possibly several references from respected members of the community. In most cases, prior to making a decision, candidates will be asked to be present for an interview. In the case of the city council or a county legislature, the interview might be with a committee or with an official from the office of the county manager or mayor. Again, in seeking an appointment, it is unwise to make promises during an interview that might be regretted at a later date. If you have not yet developed a position on a difficult issue, do not allow yourself to merely say what you think the interviewer might want to hear. Whether you are appointed or elected, you should not be encumbered by unwise commitments made during the course of a campaign.

At the end of either the appointment process or an election campaign, candidates should seek to be good losers or gracious winners. Many people fail on their first attempt at seeking a position on their local board but do succeed in subsequent efforts. Even if you are not appointed, it is still good form to send a note to thank the appropriate board for considering you. If you lose an election, it is an appropriate gesture in our democratic system to thank your supporters and to congratulate the winning candidates. For the sake of this book, we will assume that your efforts to become a board member have been successful and therefore we can now consider the preparations you should make prior to formally taking office.

NOTES

1. Virginia School Boards Association, "1999–2000 Virginia School Profile Summary," *Virginia School Boards Association Newsletter* (2000), 4.

2. "School Board Leadership," *California School Boards Association*, www.csba.org/Communications/Leadership/lead.htm (21 September 2000).

3. "How Do I Become a School Board Member? What You Should Know about School Board Service," *New York State School Boards Association*, www.nyssba.org/bdsupport/howdo2000.html (8 September 2000).

4. "$500,000 Ad Campaign Targets Trustee Zimmerman," *San Diego Union-Tribune*, 10 October 2000, 1.

CHAPTER 3

Preparing to Take Office

It is probable that you will have several weeks from the time you are elected or appointed until you take office. This is an important time when a newly elected board member should be active in learning more about the school district. Whether or not you are successful in the election, the first thing you should do is to write thank you notes to all of those who helped during the campaign. If there are some people who aided you whom you do not personally know, it is possible to take out an advertisement to thank everyone who voted for you, as well as those who helped during the campaign. Another task that is important to accomplish as soon as possible is to take down all of the signs you have spread around the district. If you have expended funds in gaining your election to the board, it is essential that all of the necessary reports outlining your use of campaign funds be submitted to the appropriate agency.

If you have not yet met the president of the board of education, or even if you have, it might be helpful to call and ask for any advice he or she might have to assist you in preparing to take office. This could include inquiring about reading materials that would aid you in learning more about your new responsibility.

Certainly, if you have not been attending regular board meetings, you should begin. As a newly elected member, you will be welcome not only at the regular public meetings but you might be invited into executive sessions and to committee meetings as well.

Many state school board associations have their own Web sites for newly elected members. Two that are particularly helpful are the New

York State Web site (www.nyssba.org) and the California State Web site (www.csba.org). The publication from the New York State School Board also includes a list of recommended reading for school board members.

The primary responsibility for orienting new members of a board of education lies with the superintendent. If your chief school officer does not contact you in the week after the election, it would be wise to make an appointment to meet. Should there be other new members, it might save time if this was done with all of the newly elected board members. An orientation meeting with the superintendent is likely to be an extended meeting; more than one session is often necessary. Prior to the meeting, it would be helpful for the board member to prepare an extended list of topics to be discussed. Along with questions, it is important to request copies of certain documents. The following outline of questions should aid you in preparing for meeting the superintendent.

1. You should request a copy of the mission statement, as well as the current goals and objectives of the school district. If, for some reason, these are not in written form, it is still an important topic for discussion. Lack of concern for such issues itself demonstrates an attitude about planning in the district.

2. It would be helpful to have a copy of the district policy manual. Such a manual should contain policies adopted by the board of education on every aspect of the school program. For example, there should be written policy in all of the following areas.
   a) *Personnel*—In this section there should be, among other things, a description of the hiring process, the plans for annual evaluations of all personnel, and seniority policies.
   b) *Use of facilities and building maintenance*—Among the matters considered in this portion of the manual would be such items as policies governing the use of school buildings by outside groups, fire inspections, and perhaps an organizational chart of the maintenance department.
   c) *Student transportation*—Policies should be in place for establishing pick-up points, bus discipline, and the use of busses by outside groups.

d) *Academic policies*—All districts should have policies on how textbooks and library books are selected and a process for dealing with complaints about books or periodicals.

e) *Field trips*—There might also be a policy governing how field trips are approved and financed.

An updated policy manual would contain guidelines on these and many other issues. If the district's policies are not available in an easy-to-use and accessible format, this can be an objective pursued by a new school board member. State school board organizations often offer sample policy statements on most topics. If the manual is nonexistent or hopelessly out of date, the assistance of a consultant could be helpful.

3. You should be sure to request copies of the school board minutes for the past year. By reading these minutes, you can follow the development of the issues that are currently facing the board. In addition, they will give you a sense of how the board spends its meeting time. Reading the minutes will offer the opportunity to judge whether they give to the reader an understandable account of what occurred at the meeting.

4. You should ask for a copy and an explanation of the organizational chart of the district. In a small district, such a chart might be given verbally; in larger districts, there will be several layers of management. If they are not contained in the policy manual, it is also helpful to obtain a copy of job descriptions. This is especially helpful for the administrative staff.

5. There should be some written procedures for board meetings. If they are not written, several questions need to be explored.

a) *Does the board function strictly under Robert's Rules of Order?* If the answer to this question is "yes," many new school board members will need to review these rules before taking office.

b) *How is the agenda for meetings determined?* What is the method a board member would use to submit items for inclusion on the agenda? Is there a deadline after which new issues cannot be added to the agenda? How soon before the meeting will you receive a copy of the agenda? What type of written backup material can you expect when you receive the agenda?

Is it possible to bring up nonagenda issues at a public meeting? Under what circumstances can this be done? Does the board conduct executive sessions (meetings where only board members and perhaps administrators are present)? Is there a law or set of rules (open meeting law) governing the topics that can be discussed in an executive session?

6. You should ask the superintendent the way he or she would suggest that you deal with complaints you receive from employees or community members. It is important to know whether you should call the superintendent directly or contact the appropriate administrator. You should also be clear as to whose responsibility it is to respond to the individual who complained.

7. It is also helpful to have an explanation of how to read the budget report, treasurer's report, and the annual audit review. As a board member, it is appropriate to have your own copy of the budget and to maintain your own records on the financial reports from the business office. The board of education is ultimately responsible for raising and monitoring the spending of public funds. Too many board members pretend that they understand the district finances but never take the time to really learn about this complex area. Most important, a new member should know about the role of the board of education in dealing with the school budget. In many communities, the school district is the largest business in the area. Board members must take their financial responsibilities seriously. This is often difficult because documents such as the annual audit report are sometimes hard to understand. One especially important portion of that report is the list of recommendations suggested by the auditor. By studying these, one can better understand any problems in the district's management of its financial affairs. Another aspect of financial management that should be watched closely is the practice of budget transfers. A budget transfer is an authorized movement of money from one budget line to another. If a large number of these transfers is repeatedly taking place, board members should question the reasons. Frequent budget transfers can be indicative of less than adequate budget forecasts or unmonitored overspending.

8. There are a number of questions that new board members should ask about the academic programs.

    a) It is important to know both the role of the state government and the school district in creating curriculum. One might inquire about the role of the board of education in curriculum matters.

    b) Another topic to ask about is how the board and the public are informed about the academic achievement levels of the students of the district.

    c) There are also several key questions to ask about the district.

    • What is the dropout rate? What has been the history of this statistic?

    • What happens to our students after they graduate? How many of them go on to college? What is the breakdown between four-year schools and community colleges? What do we know about the graduates who do not go to college?

    • What is the average class size at each grade level? Have we reduced class size in grades K–3? (Research shows that smaller classes at this level will result in increased academic achievement.)

    • How many of our students come to school with experiences in preschool programs? Does the district need to begin to consider ways to improve preschool education in the community? (Research also shows that children benefit from high-quality preschool programs.) Do we have a kindergarten screening program for children who are eligible to enter school?

    • What percentage of our children has been identified as being in need of special education services? (The national average is approximately 11 percent.) What is the role of the board of education in the area of special education? Has the district moved in the direction of including students identified as needing special education into our regular classrooms? This practice is known as inclusion.

    • Does the district have a plan for integrating technology into the academic program? What has been our progress in this area to date? Have we been establishing computer labs in each building or have we attempted to put computers in the individual classrooms? Is there an ongoing technology training program for teachers? Do we have a plan for keeping district hardware and software current?

- What is the role of the board of education concerning extracurricular activities? Do all clubs and athletic teams have to be approved by the board? Does the district have an eligibility policy for students participating in interscholastic sports and other extracurricular activities? How is the budget for these programs determined? Does the district have statistics on student participation in extracurricular activities?

9. You should also be asking questions concerning important personnel issues.

   a) It is important to have copies of labor contracts with all employee groups. In addition, it could be useful to know the timetable for negotiating future contracts with all groups.

   b) What is the role of the board of education in contract negotiations? Do board members participate actively at the negotiating table?

   c) What is the district policy for annual evaluations of all personnel? Does the board of education receive any information on these evaluations? Specifically, how does the board assess the work of the superintendent? Does the superintendent have a contract with the district? It would not be inappropriate to request a copy of the contract, although it might probably be better to wait until contract renewal discussions begin.

10. In the areas of facilities and transportation, you should request information about the current condition of the facilities. It is helpful to know about the enrollment projections and whether the current space will be adequate in the near future. You might also ask if there are any immediate plans for capital projects. If you are not aware of the geographic boundaries of the district, a map might be helpful. Another question is whether the district has its own transportation and cafeteria programs or whether these are services that are provided by independent contractors.

11. You might wish to request a copy of the school calendar. If the board meetings are not on the calendar, you should ask for a

schedule of meetings for the coming year so that you can do your best to plan on attending as many as possible. Your new responsibility as a board member is such that it is essential that these meetings have a high priority in your life.

12. One should inquire about organizations available to help new school board members. Most states have an association of school boards that sponsor conferences and conventions. Affiliation with these state organizations will provide individual board members with valuable publications, information on educational research, and sometimes even advisory legal opinions. Often there are county or regional organizations that hold informational meetings.

13. You should ask the superintendent about the board's policy with regard to the media. Should board members refer reporters to a single spokesperson, or are you free to talk openly with reporters?

14. What is the role of the school attorney? Can individual members consult with the attorney or should the superintendent or board president make such contacts?

During the orientation period, it will be helpful to seek answers to all of the questions asked above. This will not be accomplished during those few busy days before taking office. A number of meetings with the superintendent, and perhaps with the board, will certainly begin the process, but it will take some time before a new board member will really begin to feel confident in the role. Someone has suggested that during a board member's first year in office, it is expected that they will be stupid, but after that it is optional. At your first meetings with the board, it is probably wise to be a good listener and observer. Of special interest to you should be the role played by the superintendent during the meetings. Is it the style of the chief school officer to attempt to direct and control the board, or are decisions usually made because of a discussion ending in consensus? Although you might be somewhat quiet at the outset, you can never lose sight of the objectives you talked about during your campaign. As you watch the board function, you will identify the opinion leaders and the followers. When you are ready to introduce your own ideas, it is a good idea to try them out on the leaders of the board. Before introducing a major new initiative, it would also be good form to discuss the plan with the superintendent. Building support before an idea is even discussed at a meeting is important. Whether your goal is the introduction of a program for gifted and talented children, creating a lacrosse team, or adding a new foreign language, it is essential to become well informed and spend a significant amount of time talking with people whose support you will need.

Before anyone can become effective as part of any legislative body, it is essential to build trust with the other members. Be careful not to alienate your colleagues by becoming too assertive or aggressive during your initial meetings. It is also important that you avoid playing to the audience at the expense of the administration or other board members. You must always be respectful to everyone at the table as well as to the members of the community who attend board meetings. A lone maverick board member will accomplish very little if he or she is unable to gain majority support for any proposal put forward. As new members prepare to take office, they must do their homework well and then work very hard to gain the respect of their colleagues. When talking about their work as board members, it should always be "we" rather than "I." It will take some patience, but once a new member gains the trust of the administration and other board members, it is possible to emerge as a leader in a relatively short time. Besides preparing yourself by learning about your local board and community, it is also essential to begin to become aware of the major national issues involved in public education. These issues are bound at some time to touch your district. The next chapter is being included to help you better understand some of these very important topics.

CHAPTER 4

Difficult Issues

As a school board member, you will become involved with many difficult issues. Most of them will be local problems, but from time to time you will be caught up in the great national controversies. Even if you do not face these problems in your district, you will be expected as a school board member to be interested and conversant with these questions.

SCHOOL CHOICE

Over forty years ago, the conservative economist Milton Friedman began to talk and write about bringing the benefits of the free market system to education. He argued that public schools hold a near monopoly and that competition between public and private schools would force our failing public schools to improve their programs or close their doors. He was certain that competition among schools, like competition within the business community, would undoubtedly bring about a better product.

In the 1970s, the idea of choice became a reality with the creation of magnet schools in a number of communities. Districts set up a system in which individual schools would have a specific emphasis or theme. A number of large public districts, located primarily in cities, have established schools that build their curriculum around the arts, math and science, or perhaps vocational education. Other districts have created honors high schools or schools that attempted to copy what they called the "traditional school." Some districts have even experimented with single sex alternatives. In the districts that have adopted the magnet school concept, there is almost always open enrollment, but in certain cases there are entrance requirements. A school for the arts might require an audition for music candidates or an art portfolio for students wishing to major in art. An honors high school could demand a certain grade point average in junior high school as a condition for admission. In the book *Teachers, Schools, and Society*, it is pointed out that "today, more than a million students attend several thousand magnet schools."[1] Even though these schools tend to be more expensive than the neighborhood comprehensive high school, "studies suggest that they may also be more effective."[2] One danger with magnet schools is that the best music and art students, science students, and honors students would choose to attend the magnet school, leaving the remaining neighborhood schools with a large number of poorly motivated students.

A second approach to choice is the idea of open enrollment. In 1988, the state of Minnesota allowed students to seek admission to any public school they wished to attend. At least three other states have also introduced open enrollment legislation. This practice also raises problems when it is implemented. Perhaps the most difficult dilemma is in the provisions for student transportation. A state or school district considering open enrollment must decide if the school district or the parent should provide transportation. Many families could not send their children outside the neighborhood if they had to personally provide the transportation. This being the case, the option of choice would only be open to those who could afford the time and money to transport their children. On the other hand, public support for transportation that allows open enrollment can be very expensive.

By far, the most radical approach to choice is the so-called voucher system. With such a plan, the sponsoring government would give to parents, for each of their school-age children, a voucher worth a specified amount of money. These vouchers could then be taken to the public or private school chosen by the family. Supporters of the plan point out that this would give many low-income families the opportunity to send their children to private schools. They point out that in the past this option was only open to those families who could afford the tuition. It is also argued that the freedom of choice offered by the vouchers might lessen the racial segregation that has been the by-product of our neighborhood school concept. The primary argument used by those who support the plan is that the forced competition with private schools would require that the public schools become more accountable. Ineffective public schools would lose students and eventually would have to improve or be closed. This approach, which has been supported by many Republicans at both the state and national levels, was introduced in Milwaukee, Wisconsin, where every school-age child generates $3,000 that parents could use to pay for the school of their choice. This was followed by a similar plan established in Cleveland, Ohio. In 1999, the state of Florida initiated its own version of a voucher plan. This plan is currently being challenged in the courts.

The critics of vouchers include most Democrats, as well as the two major national teacher unions. Those opposed to the concept point to the fact that it could very likely be in violation of the First Amendment of the federal Constitution, which has been used by the courts to justify the separation of church and state. Another concern is the transportation problems, which would be even greater than those in an open enrollment plan, in that now parents could also choose private schools. Some critics have stated that the voucher system would not really perpetuate fair competition, as popular private schools might choose to take only the "best and brightest" students, while the more costly special education students would remain the responsibility of the public schools. Others have pointed out that competition would not necessarily foster academic excellence; rather, it would launch a flurry of spending on advertising and recruiting. It has also been noted that many parents and students choose their schools based not on the academic programs but on the sports teams and extracurricular activities that are offered. Those who oppose using vouchers for private schools suggest that these vouchers are merely a subsidy made available to those parents who are currently choosing to pay tuition for their children's education. Many of these people are already affluent and not really in need of a gift from the government. In addition, it is argued that the voucher would never be enough to pay for the total tuition of some of our more expensive private schools.

The debate will continue, although it is likely that the Supreme Court will at least rule on the constitutionality of vouchers for private schools in the near future. In Florida, Circuit Judge L. Ralph Smith ruled that the state system "violated the mandate of the Florida constitution."[3] Voucher programs have also been struck down in Ohio, Maine, Pennsylvania, and Vermont.[4] It also appears that public support of vouchers is beginning to decline. According to the 32nd Annual Phi Delta Kappa/Gallup Public's Attitudes Toward the Public Schools,

> Public willingness to experiment with attendance at private or church-related schools at public expense which increased in the late 1990s, has now peaked and seems to be declining, the report stated.

> In response to the question, "Do you favor or oppose allowing students and parents to choose a school to attend at public expense?" 39 percent in 2000 said they favor this option, a drop from . . . 44 percent in 1998, the peak year.

> Meanwhile, "public approval of the public schools is near its all-time high." According to the report, 47 percent of the general public, and 56 percent of parents with children in public schools give public schools in their community a grade of A or B. Seventy percent of parents give an A or B to the school their oldest child attends. As usual, public opinion is not nearly so favorable towards schools in abstract or those not nearby and familiar.[5]

Although the debate over vouchers is far from over, there is now a more active movement in the field of school choice. Charter schools are established by a local or state board to an individual or group to allow the operation of a publicly funded school for a specific period of time. These charter schools, although they are financed with tax dollars, are exempt from most state and local regulations. The usual exceptions would be laws or rules dealing with the health and safety of children.

An example of a typical charter school would be a situation in which a teacher or group of teachers applies for a charter to begin a school based on their own beliefs about education. A charter could also be given to a group of parents, a community group, or a private, for-profit company. The rationale for charter schools is that the independence that

the plan offers would provide those who receive a charter the freedom
to innovate. This freedom also allows schools more flexibility in hiring
teachers. Most charters allow the school to hire a percentage of uncertified instructors. Another hope is that the opportunity to choose will
cause parents and children to be more committed to and involved in
their school. Unlike the voucher plan, charter schools are all public
schools. Any application for a charter that includes specific curriculum
involving the teachings of any religious denomination would not be
approved. Even with this restriction, the number of charter schools is
increasing rapidly; currently, at least twenty states have passed laws allowing the formation of this type of school. As a rule, a charter school
typically:

- allows for the creation of a new or the conversion of an existing
  public school
- prohibits admission tests
- is nonsectarian
- requires a demonstrable improvement in performance
- can be closed if it does not meet expectations
- does not need to conform to most state rules and regulations
- receives funding based on the number of students enrolled[6]

Among the sponsors that have entered the competition for charters
are a group of profit-making companies, which have been labeled "Educational Maintenance Organizations" or EMOs. Like health maintenance organizations, it is thought that these corporations will continue
to grow in size and number. Currently, the largest is the Edison Project,
which has over fifty schools nationwide. Other well-known companies
include Tesseract and the schools begun by the Heritage Foundation.
Because EMOs and charter schools are still very new, it is too early to
gauge their success or failure. Thus far, there have been examples of
both. For a member of a school board, it is important to think about and
evaluate the various options in the choice movement. Table 4.1 attempts to highlight both the advantages and disadvantages of school
choice plans.

Table 4.1 SCHOOL BALANCE SHEET: THE SCHOOL CHOICE PLAN

Pro	Con
Free to choose from different schools (guided by their parents), children will no longer be forced to attend their neighborhood school. Education will finally be democratic.	The neighborhood school is a community of neighbors learning to work together. This is the real meaning of democracy.
Choice will lead to competition. As schools compete, they will develop their unique strengths to attract students to their programs. Without students, they will be forced to close. Only good schools will survive and prosper.	Transplanting businesslike competition into the education arena would be a disaster. False advertising, "special" promotions, a feel-good education—all the hucksterism of the marketplace—will mislead students and their parents.
The choice program will overcome the racism and classism of the neighborhood school and promote integrated schools open to all.	The choice program would deteriorate to the prejudice of private academics of the past, where race, religion, and even disability factors would be used to keep certain students from attending.
Teachers will enjoy the opportunity to leave the bureaucracy of the current system. Lifetime professionals, they will be free to create and manage their own schools.	Teachers would lose their tenure and work at the whim of the community. No professional should be forced to work from year to year without basic job security.
For the first time, poor families will be given authority to choose a school that works instead of attending neighborhood schools they know don't work. Poor Americans will be given some control over their educational futures.	Poor families would be the most victimized under a choice plan. Without education or experience, poor families are more susceptible to false advertising and misleading claims.
The choice system will increase national test scores. Schools will compete with each other academically, raising student achievement scores overall. In addition, unique types of schools will be more successful with different kinds of students.	The choice system would lower the nation's already low scores. All these different schools would teach and emphasize different topics. Without a central, accepted curricular core, fewer students would be prepared for national, standardized tests.[7]

SCHOOL VIOLENCE

Along with school choice, the issue of violence in our schools remains very much a public concern, even three years after the incident at Columbine. This is true even though statistics show that there has been a decline in violent acts in our schools.

Even though many Americans remain worried about violence in their schools, a report by the National School Safety Center pointed out that

> a school student or employee is more likely to be killed by lightning than in a school homicide. Since 1992 the annual number of children and adults who died on public or private K–12 school property or at school-sponsored events by any violent method (including suicide) ranged from 26–55 per year. . . . Meanwhile, an average of 80 Americans are killed by lightning.[8]

The same report suggests that "statistically speaking, schools are among the safest places for children to be."[9]

Despite these reports, one must be cautious in concluding that violent crime by youth will continue to decrease. In recent years, the number of young people in the age span in which there is the highest rate of crime has been down from previous generations. During the next decade, the number in this age group will increase. The nature of school violence seems also to have changed. Charles Colson wrote in a 1997 article in the *Wall Street Journal* that the new teenage criminal is "cold, remorseless, and conscienceless."[10] Others have also noted that many of the young people involved in violence in schools are careless and insensitive to the value of human life.

In responding to the well-publicized crimes of a very small minority of students, legislative bodies, including boards of education as well as the media, have spent a great deal of time attempting to pinpoint the causes of the problem. The fact that school violence has proven to be a problem in rural and suburban schools, along with schools in the urban setting, has made this a national issue. Blame has been laid on the media for their violent programming, which many have charged is targeted to young people. Others have pointed to violent computer and video games. New laws to increase gun control have also been pursued. In an effort to keep guns away from unbalanced young people all over the country, stricter penalties have been passed to punish those who bring weapons on school grounds.

Perhaps the most common reaction of school boards has been the introduction of new security measures. Thousands of security guards have been hired to patrol the halls of our schools. Metal detectors have been introduced to some communities in an attempt to stop those who might bring weapons to school. Doors are kept locked and students, staff, and faculty are required to wear nametags. Some districts have put in closed circuit television cameras to allow security guards to see what is going on throughout the building. After-school events are also closely monitored. In schools all over the country, "breath tests" have been instituted at the school dances. Any student found to be intoxicated would not be allowed to enter the dance and could be suspended from school.

To keep order on school buses, aides have been employed to help maintain discipline. Other districts have aimed video cameras at the students riding on the bus in an attempt to record infractions of bus conduct rules.

All of these responses are honest efforts by schools to provide security and safety for their students. Still, some critics, including many students, have charged that we are making our schools more and more like prisons and that we have avoided serious efforts to deal with the underlying student alienation that is the cause of the violence. They point out the need to offer help to those students who feel ostracized by their peers. Pointing to the recent perpetrators of school violence, the critics suggest that these students were isolated and unhappy young people who were being ignored by the adults who could help them. It is frequently argued that schools should have in place ways to identify potential problem students. Some schools have attempted to train school personnel to discover the identity of troubled young people. At the same time, it is essential that there be adults in the school and community who can act as counselors and mentors for "at-risk children." Too many students have no adult with whom they can comfortably speak about their troubles. Unfortunately, many parents are not filling this role, nor are our school guidance counselors. A number of schools have hired informal counselors whose only duty is to be available to troubled youth. Other schools have attempted peer mediation of conflicts as a way to deal with serious problems. There is also experimentation taking place with projects that have senior high mentors working with middle school students.

Another aspect of the problem is breaking the code of silence among teenagers. Anyone who has ever worked in a secondary school knows that students are very reticent to talk with adults about their peers. To begin to break the code of silence, a school needs some basic plans in place, including:

- A character education program that emphasizes the values of courage, caring, and responsibility. Emphasizing these values helps students better understand that staying silent in the face of potential danger is cowardly, uncaring, and irresponsible.
- Regular discussions of the school discipline code. You can't just hand out student handbooks at the beginning of the school year and hope the kids will review the discipline code. Teachers should be given extra time to discuss the rules and consequences in the school discipline code with students.
- A formal discussion about safety and security with parents, preferably held at school open house meetings. These meetings present an excellent opportunity because they are one of the few times during the year when the school is packed with parents. Parents need to know they play an important role in helping ensure the safety of all students in the school.
- A twenty-four-hour, seven-days-a-week telephone hotline students and parents can use to report potential danger in or near the school—but you cannot simply install a phone line and hope people will call. The number needs to be promoted and marketed in school and community newsletters and local newspapers. Teachers and principals need to promote the number inside the school by placing posters in the hallways and in their rooms, and they need to make sure students understand that their calls will be confidential.
- An established protocol for responding to reports of potential violence.[11]

Schools alone cannot solve the problem of violence in our society. Church groups, the Boy Scouts and Girl Scouts, community athletic programs, and other youth organizations must reach out to the students at risk. Too often, our church youth groups and other organizations are closed societies that make little or no effort to recruit those who are alienated or just lonely.

No single solution will make our schools safer. Still, it is essential that boards of education go beyond instituting more and more security measures. Schools and communities must attempt to find ways to deal with the underlying causes of the problem.

THE STANDARDS MOVEMENT

A third major issue that will undoubtedly face school board members during the next decade is the standards movement and its reliance on "high-stakes testing." We are currently in a period of educational reform, which many believe began in 1983 with the report entitled "The Nation at Risk: The Imperative for Educational Reform." As a result of this and other national reports published in the mid-1980s, major changes including the following, occurred in the schools.

- Nearly 300 local and state panels were formed.
- More than forty states increased course requirements for graduation.
- Thirty-three states instituted testing for student promotion or graduation.
- More than 700 state statutes were passed stipulating what should be taught, when it should be taught, how it should be taught, and who should do the teaching.
- Almost half the states passed legislation to increase qualification standards and pay for teachers.
- Most states increased the length of the school day and/or school year.
- Most states passed laws that required teachers and students to demonstrate computer literacy.[12]

At the same time these changes were taking place, the Bush administration established commissions of experts in various curriculum areas to create national education standards. The controversial reports of these groups listed what the authors believed students throughout the United States should know and be able to do in a number of subject areas. Although the idea of a national curriculum failed to generate political support, the idea of establishing curricular standards spread to many state governments. For some of these efforts, the national standards were a guide, but most states seemed to go their own way. As these new state standards were introduced in the 1990s, there was at the same time a call for increased accountability for our schools. Most states responded by establishing higher graduation requirements and a statewide testing program. The results of these new examinations we to be made known to the public. States are increasingly mandating "school report cards," which allow district residents to gauge and compare the success of the school's academic program. When a school district's scores are in a period of decline, one can expect a very vocal reaction within the community. The local media, as well as school district newsletters, report these results. Angry parents, teachers under pressure, and fearful administrators are struggling to develop programs that will bring up test scores. The intensity of the pressures have resulted in several well-publicized situations in which teachers and administrators have been found to have cheated in order to ensure high test scores. In California, eighteen schools were disqualified from receiving thousands of dollars for top scorers on the state's basic skills exam.[13] New York City has also been the scene of a large cheating scandal that included a number of teachers and principals. Critics of the push for higher standards and more testing have already emerged. One argument put forward by the dissenters is that the charge that the schools of the United States are failing is not necessarily true. The *Sacramento Bee* published an editorial on September 10, 2000, entitled "Fresh Look at Schools: They Aren't Doing As Badly As Many Think." The article quotes a report of the Brown Conference on American Education that stated that between 1971 and 1999, reading scores of ninth graders increased from 208 to 212, while in math the scores went from 219 to 232 on tests where the range was from zero to five hundred. For all age groups, the math scores registered in 1999 by our students were the best in the history of the test.[14] The report went on to state that "The story is not one of disastrous decline. It is instead a tale of baby steps forward. And while baby steps may not be occasion for much celebration, they are striking for the context in which they've occurred: a time when child poverty, single-parent households and non-English speaking students were increasing dramatically."[15]

The possibility that schools are not as bad as the critics claim should not be enough to slow the movement for higher academic standards. What could slow the movement is a significant uprising by parents and students. On September 28, 2000, the Associated Press carried a story with the headline "Parents Mobilize Nationwide to Fight Standardized Tests."[16] A national organization called the National Center for Fair and

..sting, located in Cambridge, Massachusetts, is leading the
This and other groups throughout the country are arguing that
..e exams place too much stress on children, miscalculate their abilities, limit what they are taught, and weigh too much in determining whether they are held back."[17]

Other critics point to the fact that the creativity of teachers is being limited as they are forced to "teach for the test." Some instructors complain that the need to "cover the material" reduces the possibility of in-depth discussion of issues that is so important to students. Projects and cooperative learning must be curtailed because of the need to have long review sessions. Some teachers have canceled field trips and other projects that were popular activities for children. Teachers also complain that all administrators care about is the test results. The result of this unrest is causing a number of states to ease the requirements of their testing programs. This seems to be the case in Maryland, Virginia, and Louisiana.[18]

An article in *Education Week* includes the arguments of those who are concerned with our national addiction to testing. Entitled "Weighing the Cattle Doesn't Make Them Fatter," the author asks the question, "Is a public shaming really needed for accountability?" The author, Suzanne Tingley, a school superintendent in New York State, concludes her article: "underlying all of this testing, of course, there is the presumption that schools won't do the job unless they are publicly shamed into it. This is not only an insult to the majority of professional educators, it is simply untrue."[19] On the other hand, the author notes that our society needs to understand the following truths.

- The majority of teachers care about kids and are doing a good job.
- The majority of kids trust their teachers and want to come to school.
- Beating up schools in the media will not improve education.
- Arduous and frequent testing does not make kids smarter.[20]

Despite this movement to lessen the pressures of "high-stakes" testing, this issue will not disappear during the next decade. With this in mind, it would be helpful to consider what schools can do to increase the academic achievement of its students. There are several actions that would be verified by significant bodies of research.

1. We must do a better job in making quality preschool programs available to every family regardless of their income levels. Students are now entering kindergarten with vastly different degrees of readiness. Some students are already reading while others have not begun to learn the alphabet. Communities are failing to offer their children equal educational opportunities if only some are able to benefit from quality preschool education.

2. It is widely accepted that reducing class size in grades K–3 will have a long-term effect on student learning. As a result, many states, including California and New York, have established major incentives for districts to lower the teacher-pupil ratio in the lower grades. The results of a massive study on student achievement rates in Tennessee and in other places validate the effectiveness of such an approach.[21]

3. There is a growing number of studies that suggest that the social and academic benefits of smaller schools are considerable. As a result, some districts that have built buildings for thousands of students are creating "schools within a school." In doing so, they assign specific faculty members and administrators to deal with a smaller number of students. It is the hope that they will be able to create additional school spirit and a sense of community within this smaller organization.

4. Spending money on appropriate teacher in-service training also appears to be a good investment. Such programs must be more than occasional inspirational speakers. In-service training for all faculty and staff should be, for the most part, concerned with what these people do each working day. It must be ongoing and offer opportunities for individual faculty members to try out new techniques under the supervision of experts. Establishing mentor programs for new teachers also can reduce the number of faculty members who leave their position after a year or two. The guidance of a seasoned veteran can be invaluable to new teachers. Even if a district has to pay mentors, it can be worth the money. Staff development opportunities are also necessary

as schools attempt to introduce technology into the academic programs. Older faculty members must be taught ways to effectively use the computers that are being provided for their classrooms.

5. It is widely agreed that increasing the amount of time that students are actually engaged in instruction can only help to bolster student achievement. Districts all over the country are seeking ways to gain more instructional time. Adding minutes to the school day or days to the school calendar are only two of the approaches being attempted. Review and remedial classes as well as after- and before-school hours are being used. Extensive summer programs for children failing to meet the required standards are also being established. One of the popular approaches at the secondary level is to convert the traditional eight forty-five-minute period schedule into what is called a block schedule. Under such a plan, classes meet less often but in larger time blocks. Longer periods are especially helpful in science classes, as the lecture and lab portion of the classes can take place during the same day. When teachers employ a variety of teaching strategies for the longer classes, students appear to support the idea of block scheduling. Another possible positive outcome can be a reduction in what is often wasted time in study halls. Changing the schedule itself is not likely to dramatically improve student learning, but it can have some positive results. Block scheduling might be especially helpful if it is difficult or impossible to add time to the instructional day or days to the calendar. Most often, this cannot be done unless the district is willing to pay extra money to the faculty and staff. In the end, increasing the amount of time students and teachers are actively engaged in instruction is probably one of the most effective ways to raise academic standards.

6. Another major factor that will insure the success of schools is the ability of the district to recruit the best possible teachers and administrators. Although teachers are obviously the key to success, the Effective School Research that was done during the 1970s pointed to the importance of the building principal. A leader who is able to communicate a clear vision for the school and successfully provide a wholesome and safe educational environment will help to ensure an effective school. At the same time, the principal

needs to be the instructional leader in the building. Too many of our building principals spend most of their time on student discipline and the mechanics of managing the building. In choosing a principal, the board of education needs to select someone who understands teaching and has a commitment to improving instruction. Even the best principal cannot ensure an effective school without a well-prepared and committed faculty. Board members should insist that the district have a personnel program that recruits and works to keep quality teachers. Board members must resist the temptation to pressure administrators to hire local candidates who happen to be friends or acquaintances. Before approving new appointments or recommendations for tenure, the board should insist on being given background material on the teachers in question and also be given the opportunity to ask questions about administrative recommendations.

All of these suggestions can help a board in its search for ways to increase student achievement. Many boards of education seldom spend significant amounts of time discussing instructional issues. Instead, meeting time is only used to talk about the business aspects of the school district. This is unfortunate; as an individual board member, you should urge that the agenda include time for discussing academic questions. One way to achieve this type of focus is to invite groups of teachers to board meetings to report on their programs. Once placed on the agenda, there should be sufficient time allotted for informal conversation between board members and the visiting delegation. Teachers appreciate it when the board of education demonstrates a sincere interest in their work. A secondary benefit of such interaction is that it helps school employees to see that board members are real people who truly care about the children attending the district's schools. Unfortunately, in some districts, many employees view the board of education as only being interested in lowering the tax rate. Although it does not happen often, some school administrators blame the board of education for any unpopular decision that is made within the district. By meeting occasionally with faculty members, you can become more personally involved and better understand the academic program of the school district.

The National School Boards Association published the following checklist to help school board members decide if their board is adequately focusing their attention on student achievement.

- Our school board meetings are focused on issues related to student achievement.
- Our board has led or facilitated conversations in our community that have helped set a common vision for student achievement and a clear definition of student success.
- Our board uses reliable data to make informed decisions about how to support student achievement goals and how to measure progress.
- Our board acts to bring diverse opinions to bear and create community consensus on student achievement goals.
- Our board sets benchmarks and discusses progress toward student achievement goals.
- Our board and superintendent play a leadership role in defining standards of achievement for all students.
- Our board has developed a process for maintaining accountability within the schools, the district office, and the school board itself.
- Our board-superintendent team, in board meetings and in its relation to the district, models teamwork and partnership for the schools and the community.
- Our board has established mechanisms for feedback from parents, administrators, teachers, and the greater community regarding student achievement goals.
- Our board works to create policies that clearly support the student achievement goals.[22]

OTHER ISSUES

Religion

It would be wonderful if boards of education were able to spend most of their time on academic matters; unfortunately, other issues are likely to intrude. One such issue that can quickly divide a community is the proper relationship between schools and religion. The current law in this very controversial area is primarily the result of a series of cases before the federal judiciary. In all of these cases, the courts have been attempting to interpret two seemingly simple phrases from the First Amendment of the United States Constitution. The first phrase is: "Congress shall make no law respecting an establishment of religion," and the second prohibits the government from interfering with the free exercise of religion.[23] During the twentieth century, the federal courts have created an ever-changing body of case law that provides the guidelines for public schools as they seek to establish a legal relationship with the many varied religious groups in our society.

It is not the purpose of this book to summarize or explain all of the judicial decisions that have shaped the current relationship between church and state in this country. Still, it seems important to caution board members on the variety of potential legal issues that could ensnarl a district in this very emotional area.

Perhaps the place to begin this discussion is in a consideration of the curriculum. The dispute between those who support the teaching of Darwin's theory of evolution and the religious conservatives who seek the inclusion in the curriculum of the creation theory continues into the twenty-first century. Having first captured the imagination of the nation in the Scopes trial in 1925, the issue will not die. As a result, it could still be raised for discussion in any community.

Health classes also provide an arena for those who oppose sex education, especially if it includes instruction in birth control. A health teacher who invites a representative from Planned Parenthood to speak to the class can ignite angry criticism from those who oppose abortion. This could occur whether or not the speaker even talks about abortion.

Selection of books and other materials can also lead to controversy. A single sentence or paragraph in a library book or textbook which appears to be critical of someone's faith can lead to heated requests for banning the material in the school. It is essential that districts have a clear and legally defensible policy for dealing with complaints on any learning activity, curriculum material, or library book. Sample policies can be acquired from any state school board association or from a neighboring district.

Prayer at public events can be another source of conflict within a district. Currently, the courts and the United States Department of Education have provided some guidelines in this area. A student-led, nondenominational prayer can be included in a graduation ceremony if the students involved have approved of the decision. A recent Supreme Court decision, however, declared unconstitutional a student-led prayer before a high school football game. As a result, the question of school prayer at public events is currently somewhat unclear. What the courts have said is that public prayer at school events cannot be led by clergy or school personnel. Board members and administrators must attempt to continue to follow carefully court decisions relating to this matter.

The responsibility of public school districts regarding the parochial schools in their community is also undergoing change. Court decisions have made clear that district funds must be used to provide transportation to religious schools that are a certain distance from the district's public school. It is also clear that tax dollars can be used to purchase textbooks and other learning materials for religious-based schools. The public school district in the community must also pay for health services, remedial classes, special education, as well as vocational education for parochial schools. Recently, the courts have upheld the practice of public schools giving to religious-based schools unneeded instructional equipment, such as computers. Again, in this area of the law, it is important for districts to remain current.

Another issue is the question of the use of school buildings by religious groups. Presently, under restricted conditions, students can hold prayer groups and Bible study classes in a public school building. It is also true that schools must, upon request, grant churches the right to have one hour a week for religious education, but such classes cannot be held in a public building.

The celebration of holidays in schools has created controversy in many communities. Disputes have arisen over singing Christmas carols at the holiday concert and more recently there have been problems concerning the celebration of Halloween in school. School officials must be sensitive to minority concerns in these matters and listen carefully to the protestors. The celebration of religious holidays in public schools has been addressed in a publication entitled "Religious Holidays in the Public Schools, Questions and Answers," which is available online at www.osba-ohio.org/Holidays.html.

With all of the issues, board members should insist that the district seek a legal opinion prior to making a decision on a controversial church and state matter. Going to court can not only divide a community but can also be very costly to the school district. Since most local school attorneys are not experts in constitutional law, it is often wise to consult the legal division of your state or the National School Boards Association. Even though this type of issue can involve a board member's personal religious convictions, any decision should be based on the law, as well as what is best for the children of the district. Often, a nasty confrontation can be avoided if the school district makes an effort to meet and listen to the unhappy citizens who are bringing the complaint.

Sexual Discrimination

An additional issue that is likely to come to the forefront in the near future is the question of how schools will deal with homosexual students and job candidates. Homosexual students have sued or threatened to sue in a number of school districts for the right to meet on school property. Even though hundreds of schools have permitted such clubs to hold their meetings in a classroom, other districts have refused and found themselves embroiled in a public and sometimes legal controversy. The New York State School Boards Association published the following list of considerations when determining whether any student-initiated club should be allowed to meet in a district room.

- Does the proposed club fit the mold of what the Federal Equal Access Act is intended to protect? That is, could it be construed as political, religious, or philosophical in nature?
- Is there someone willing to monitor the club? For safety and security reasons, you need to ensure that an adult is monitoring the group.
- Have you overstepped your boundaries? Arbitrarily picking and choosing clubs to deem acceptable is illegal.
- Have you examined your policy? Ensure that your decisions regarding controversial clubs have been consistent with your written policy on the subject.
- Can you say with certainty that the club could cause material and substantial classroom disruption?[24]

Along with the rights of homosexual students, a board could also find itself facing questions involving homosexuals on their current staff or as new job applicants. Although federal law does not currently protect homosexuals from discrimination in the same way that racial minorities and women are protected, it is possible that such a law will be passed in the near future. Some states and local communities already prohibit discrimination based on sexual preference. In some communities, hiring a professed homosexual would not be a particularly controversial issue. In other, more conservative areas, it could create a problem. A similar dilemma could arise at the time of the tenure vote for a known homosexual. When forced to vote on such an issue, board members should consider not only the law but also their own conscience.

Academic Grouping

Academic grouping is a major issue that continues to be a source of controversy in our schools. For much of the twentieth century, tracking students in classes with children of similar academic ability has been an accepted practice. There have been numerous varieties of academic grouping, both at the elementary and secondary level. In the elementary schools, students of mixed ability are often assigned to the same teacher. During the school day, the teacher might work with a small reading group while assigning the rest of the class to do seat work. A more complex system of ability grouping is to have elementary students move from classroom to classroom within the grade level for all subjects. In such situations, the elementary child could have several different teachers during the day, depending on academic grouping. The third and most rigid method is to divide the students at a particular grade level by academic ability and have these students stay together with one teacher for the entire day. If the grade level has a hundred students and four teachers, the top twenty five students would be assigned to teacher A, the next academic group to teacher B, and so on.

At the secondary level, we have long divided students either by subject or, in some cases, young people stay in the same group for all of their subjects. In recent years, it has been more common for some students to be in the top group for certain subjects, but not necessarily in all curriculum areas. In addition, high schools have developed special honor programs and advanced placement options (college credit courses) for more able students.

During the past decade, academic grouping has been under attack on many fronts. Critics have charged that schools and teachers have lower expectations and are less concerned about lower-track students. These classes sometimes have been plagued with discipline problems as well as poor academic achievement. At the same time, the standards movement has argued that all students should be challenged to meet higher academic expectations. These issues, along with the possible damage that grouping has done to the self-esteem of slower students, have caused many parents and educators to question the practice of academic grouping. Some observers have noted that grouping can also lead to social cliques within a school. Others have argued that having classes containing students of mixed ability also allows for the possibility of peer teaching. Simultaneously, parents of special education students, government officials, and judges have pushed schools into including in the regular classroom students who had previously been placed in self-contained special education classrooms. All of these factors have created a national trend away from academic grouping. The practice of "detracking" schools has led to great challenges for teachers.

The movement to modify or eliminate academic grouping has not been accepted by all teachers and parents. There is the feeling among some of these critics that heterogeneous grouping is holding back the more able students. As the debate rages, the research on grouping offers evidence on both sides of the issue. The practice labeled inclusion, which is moving handicapped students from self-contained special education classrooms into regular classrooms, is a trend that is affecting schools all over the country. Public Law 94-142, as passed in 1975, stated that students who were judged in need of special education should be assigned in the "least restricted environment." Even with this warning, many districts throughout the country placed these special education students in separate classrooms, often in schools or institutions that were located a distance from the child's home. Because of pressure from some of the parents of these students and the resulting support of the courts and state education departments, many of these students are being reassigned to regular classrooms. Special education teachers who once taught their own small group of classified children have become part of a team with the regular classroom teachers and other specialists. Children who are deaf, blind, physically handicapped, and even some who are mentally retarded or emotionally disturbed now can be found in a regular classroom. Although these students might be "pulled out" during the school day for special services, such as counseling or speech or physical therapy, they may spend a majority of their time with students who have not been classified as needing special education. This practice of inclusion appears to be having very positive results for the academic and social growth of those children classified as special education students. Inclusion has the added social benefit of exposing other children to peers who have disabilities in the hope that this experience will make children more sensitive and tolerant to those who are different. The differentiated instruction required in the inclusive classrooms is also opening up new and creative ways of teaching.

At the same time that many are championing inclusion, there are those who talk about the confusion and disruption that the practice can bring to a classroom. Others worry about the fact that sometimes children are not accepting and are often cruel to the new students in their classroom. Board members will be asked to approve the recommendations of the special education committee of their districts. They will also vote on expenditures made to implement the special education program of the district. Nationwide, approximately 11 percent of students are receiving special educational services. Much of the increase in school spending during the past three decades has resulted from the added expenses of these programs. There are those who believe that we are spending too much on this minority of students and shortchanging the remainder of the student body. These are questions that every board will be asked to face.

A related grouping issue, which continues to be a subject of discussion in many districts, is the question of specific programs for gifted students. In dealing with this question, the first problem a board of education must face is determining how to identify those students who should participate in a program for the gifted. Should teachers be the primary source of referral? Another method is to merely use IQ scores as a screening device. Can parents petition to have their children included? Will the definition of gifted include children with special talents in specific areas? If so, such programs will be made available to both the academically gifted and those with special talents.

Assuming that a district can agree on a screening process, the next decision is to choose an appropriate way to provide the services. A number of options can be considered. At the elementary school level, one alternative is to have a "pull-out" program where a specially assigned teacher of the gifted and talented meets for several hours a week with the selected students during the school day. These sessions are used to engage the children in challenging and creative projects that supplement the curriculum at their grade level. Other schools have chosen to hire an "enrichment teacher," who works as a consultant with all of the classroom teachers to carry out projects that give special opportunities to all of the classes in the school. The advantage of this approach is that it provides enriched learning for all students. Still other communities provide Saturday or summer classes that are open to students who wish to study specific topics in depth. Often, these offerings are made available by local colleges either during the school year or during the summer. Unfortunately, unless the school district picks up the cost, these special opportunities are only open to those families who can afford the tuition. Academic competitions such as "Masterminds" or "Olympics of the Mind" also offer a way to challenge gifted students. Traditionally, some school districts have also considered acceleration as an option for very able students. A child might be advanced an entire grade level or in a secondary school would skip one level of a class in certain subjects. It is not unusual for a student to be allowed to take ninth-grade math during the eighth-grade year. Of course, when considering acceleration, schools must take into account the social implications of the move for the student in question.

At the high school level, the introduction of challenging advanced placement courses allows able students to receive college credit while attending high school. In some communities, high school seniors are actually attending classes during part of their day at a nearby college campus.

Depending on the school district, board members can expect that there will be an articulate and insistent group of parents seeking new programs for gifted and talented students. They will point to studies showing that many of these students are bored with school and are not meeting their academic potential. There is also evidence that gifted and talented students might be more likely to turn to drugs or even suicide. These parents will talk about the wasted potential of our future scientists, doctors, and leaders. Often, the argument is raised that we are spending huge amounts of money on special education but paying little or no attention to the needs of the gifted and talented. Board members will quickly become aware that their district is receiving significant amounts of governmental aid for special education students but little or none for gifted and talented programs. The history of this issue in many districts is that when money becomes short, gifted and talented programs are among the first to be cut. Board members faced with this type of decision should ask for any relevant research on the educational value of some programs.

Employee Compensation

Another issue likely to arise during your tenure as a board member is merit pay, or performance-based compensation, for teachers and other school employees, which has long been a policy supported by many board members. Coming from private industry where workers' salary increases are based in large part upon the evaluation of their managers, board members feel that school employees might be motivated to work even harder if their pay was based on their performance. Although in recent years a number of teachers' unions have accepted contracts that contain limited merit provisions, the position of most teacher unions is to oppose the concept. Often, it is argued that teaching is an art and that a teacher's performance cannot easily be quantified. Attempts to do so often rely heavily on student achievement. Teachers will likely point out that their job includes much more than preparing students for tests. In addition, the results frequently depend on the attitude and aptitude of the students assigned to the teacher. Other methods of deciding merit are equally suspect. Many teachers do not trust school administrators to judge their work based on a minimal number of classroom observations. Too often, they point out, the principal or other supervisor knows little about the subject being taught and has little or no knowledge of the particular students in the classroom. Peer evaluation of a teacher's work can create conflict within the faculty and might well be affected by friendships among the teachers in the school. This, like many other issues, will continue to be discussed and one can hope that teacher unions and boards of education will find ways to reward good teaching. Still, new board members should know at the outset that any effort to introduce a compensation system based on performance will require long and careful negotiations with employee groups and that the effort might well result in frustration and failure.

Site-Based Management

More than ever, employee groups, as well as parents, are seeking additional input into decision making in our public schools. This desire, along with some significant educational research, has led to a trend labeled "site-based management." The theory is that school districts allowing increased autonomy for decision making at the individual school level will end up with both better decisions and improved morale. Supporters have argued that those working at the individual building level are in a better position to judge the needs of the students in their building. Committees made up of the principal, parents, teachers, and sometimes students have been given the power to make recommendations to initiate school policy, aid in budget decisions, and in some cases, participate in the hiring procedure. Some states have actually mandated the formation of these site-based committees. The results of this trend have been mixed. Building principals sometimes feel that their authority is being reduced as they are forced to accept decisions made by consensus. Boards of education are not always willing to implement the recommendations of the committees, thus causing frustration among the members of the site-based management committee. Taken as a whole, it would seem that the trend toward using advisory committees and allowing more decisions to be made at the building level is likely to continue. Certainly, in establishing such groups, a board must clearly define their mission and their powers. It must be made clear that most groups will be mainly advisory and that the final decisions will rest with the board of education.

Language Education

There is another issue that also has been the subject of numerous school board meetings during the past several decades. The question of how best to teach language skills has become the source of an emotional and ongoing conflict in our schools. Before the emergence of the whole language approach, students were taught with a basal reader, along with workbooks emphasizing grammar and punctuation. A separate book was used to teach spelling, and composition was usually taught as a separate skill from reading. The heart of the reading program was a word decoding system known as phonics. In her recent book on the history of American education, Diane Ravitch writes that "whole language was a rebellion against drill, workbooks, textbooks, and the other paraphernalia associated with phonics that, overdone, could deaden students interest in reading."[25]

The concept of whole language has been described in many ways. One textbook defines it as "teaching reading through an integration of language arts skills and knowledge, with a heavy emphasis on literature (as contrasted with a phonics approach)."[26] As it spread across the country, workshops were held on whole language in every section of the United States. Schools were urged to develop their own classroom libraries of outstanding children's books. Oversized books, labeled "big books," were purchased in large numbers. These books were considered quality children's literature, which would create a high interest level among the students. They sometimes replaced the basal reader series and were used to provide a combined approach to language arts instruction. Instead of separate spelling books, student's spelling words were taken from the literature they were reading. The same is true with compositions or writing assignments. Many believe that children learn to write best by being given many high interest and creative assignments. In the early grades, students were not to be frustrated by too many teacher corrections. Many teachers accept "creative spelling" in order not to stifle their student's excitement about writing. Some school districts went so far in their adoption of the whole language philosophy that they ceased to use basal reading series and relied solely on a literature-based language arts program. A number of educators accepted the idea that if students read enough books and used context clues in decoding unknown words, the dreaded instruction in phonetics could be reduced or eliminated.

After some rather extensive testing in the late 1990s, a cloud began to form over the extensive use of the whole language method. The state of California, which had moved strongly in the direction of whole language instruction in the late 1980s and early 1990s, saw its reading scores plummet to the point where student reading achievement compared unfavorably with the rest of the country. There was a widespread political movement that emphasized the need to return to the use of phonetic education. Supporters of the whole language movement pointed to the fact that reading scores had declined not because of the teaching methods employed in the schools, but rather because Proposition 13 had dramatically reduced educational spending. The severe financial restrictions during this period had led to large increases in class size. These, coupled with the huge influx of non-English speaking children, were the real culprits in causing the lower reading scores, according to the whole language supporters. In any case, California brought phonics back into the required curriculum prescribed by the State of California Education Department. The teaching of phonics has also increased in many other school districts when it appeared in the late 1990s that a consensus was emerging about how to teach reading. Studies reinforced earlier research that had shown that the best language arts programs combined the traditional phonics approach with many of the ideas associated with whole language instruction. Still, as we enter the twenty-first century, the debate continues. As 1999 ended, the annual meeting of the Council of Teachers of English passed a resolution that opposed phonics instruction. It seems clear that we have not yet put to rest the argument as to how best to teach reading.

Reading instruction, like the other issues discussed in this chapter, will be among those that will engage future board members. Although you will grapple with many such problems during your years of service, no single decision will be more important for your local district than the selection of a new superintendent. For that reason, the chapter that follows will be devoted to this all-important task.

NOTES

1. Myra Pollack Sadker and David Miller Sadker, *Teachers, Schools, & Society* (Boston: McGraw-Hill, 2000), 153.

2. Sadker and Sadker, *Teachers, Schools, & Society*, 153.

3. "Florida Statewide Voucher Program Ruled Unconstitutional," Illinois Association of School Boards 2000, www.iasb.com/files/nb0400.htm (9 October 2000).

4. Illinois Association of School Boards.

5. "Gallup Poll Shows Public Support for Vouchers Declining," Illinois Association of School Boards 2000, www.iasb.com/files/nb0900.htm (9 October 2000).

6. Sadker and Sadker, *Teachers, Schools, & Society*, 156.

7. Sadker and Sadker, *Teachers, Schools, & Society*, 161.

8. "After Columbine, Schools Focus on Improving Safety," New York State School Boards Association 2000, www.nyssba.org/adnews/issues/issues052200.2.html (10 August 2000).

9. New York State School Boards Association.

10. Wolfgang W. Halbig, "Breaking the Code of Silence," *National School Boards Association American School Board Journal*, March 2000, www.asbj.com/security/contents/0300halbig.html (22 September 2000).

11. Halbig, "Breaking the Code."

12. Sadker and Sadker, *Teachers, Schools, & Society*, 149.

13. Susan Gembrowski, "18 Schools Lose State Funds," *San Diego Union-Tribune*, 5 October 2000, www.sandi.net/comm/articles/uniontrib/ut.001005.funds.htm (19 October 2000).

14. "Fresh Look at Schools: They Aren't Doing As Badly As Many Think," *Sacramento Bee*, 10 September 2000, www.sacbee.com.com/voices/news/old/voices01_000910.html (19 October 2000).

15. "Fresh Look."

16. Associated Press, "Parents Mobilize Nationwide to Fight Standardized Test," *Batavia Daily News*, 28 September 2000, 6 (B).

17. "Parents Mobilize."

18. National School Boards Association, "Some States Are Easing High-Stake Testing Strategies," *School Board News*, 30 May 2000, www.nsba.org/sbn/00-may/050300-3.htm (2000).

19. Suzanne Tingley, "Weighing the Cattle Doesn't Make Them Fatter," Virginia School Board Association, reprinted from *Education Week*, April 2000.

20. Tingley, "Weighing the Cattle."

21. Nancy L. Waymack and Darrel W. Drury, "Sizing It Right," *National School Boards Association* 1, no. 1 (summer/fall 1999): 1–4.

22. National School Boards Association, reprinted in the Illinois Association of School Boards *School Board News Bulletin*, May 2000, www.iasb.com/files/nb0500.htm (9 October 2000).

23. John D. Hicks and George E. Mowry, *A Short History of American Democracy* (Boston: Houghton Mifflin, 1956), x.

24. National School Boards Association, *Your School and the Law Newsletter*, 17 January 2000, 4.

25. Diane Ravitch, *Left Back: A Century of Failed School Reforms* (New York: Simon & Schuster, 2000), 443.

26. Sadker and Sadker, *Teachers, Schools, & Society*, 570.

CHAPTER 5

Choosing a Superintendent

For boards of education, the challenge of finding the right superintendent for their districts may never have been more difficult. Numerous sources have documented the fact that fewer qualified candidates for the position are available than in the past. The Virginia School Board Newsletter recently published an article entitled "Superintendent Shortage May Be Reaching Crisis Stages." Taken from the National School Boards Association News Service, it states that

> school superintendents are becoming an endangered species, with fewer people seeking these high-stress jobs, reports a new study by the American Association of School Administrators (AASA). According to the forthcoming *Career Crisis in the Superintendency*, 80 percent of superintendents are at or near the age of retirement. Nearly 70 percent of those surveyed were between 50 and 59 years of age, and almost 11 percent were 60 or older.[1]

The problem appears greatest in our cities, where in April 2000, "at least thirteen large urban school districts, including New York and Los Angeles, were looking for school chiefs."[2]

Another source pointed out the domino effect on middle-management positions as lower-level managers are appointed as replacements for superintendents. The need for principals and other district administrators will also be great, as 38 percent of the chief school officers are chosen from within the organization.[3] The high turnover rate among all school administrators makes it necessary that school boards pay careful attention to both finding and keeping outstanding administrators for their district.

There are some suggestions that have been made to help deal with the shortage of candidates. The Connecticut Association of Boards of Education cooperated with other agencies to publish a document entitled "Leadership under Pressure." The authors list the following recommendations to deal with the crisis in the superintendency.

- Local, regional, and state agencies should agree on the nature and extent of the shortage and cooperate on resolving the problem.
- School boards and superintendents should redefine their roles, rights, and responsibilities. Superintendents should have final authority for personnel and other matters for which they are accountable.
- More needs to be done to increase opportunities for women and minorities.
- States should improve and fund certification preparation and training opportunities for superintendents.
- The position of superintendent should be made more manageable, more attractive, and more secure.
- Action needs to be taken to allow certification and pension portability among states.
- Talented leaders should be identified early and given high-powered training to groom them for leadership positions.
- Salary and benefit issues need to be addressed. The study notes the small differential between the superintendent's salary and that of educators and principals deters many from seeking the high-pressured, more demanding job of superintendent.
- Additional ways need to be found to recognize and celebrate superintendents.[4]

These suggestions might help solve the problem in the long run, but meanwhile hundreds of boards of education across the country will be facing the task of choosing a new superintendent during the near future. Although the process varies depending on the location and the size of the community, there will be a number of steps that will be necessary for any district. When a vacancy occurs, the first place a board of education will look is within the organization. If there is an assistant superintendent or building principal who has the enthusiastic support of all of the board members, it probably will not be necessary to develop a search strategy. In some districts, there is an individual who has been groomed for the position and the selection is almost automatic. In making this type of appointment, a board must be certain that this person has strong support not only from board members but also from the faculty, staff, and community. If it is not obvious to all that such support exists, the board should not make a quick decision. An inside candidate chosen without the enthusiastic endorsement of all of the constituencies of the district could have difficulty meeting the challenges of the position. On the other hand, if an administrator has sufficient experience and a relatively high level of support, he or she could be appointed as interim superintendent during the search process. Allowing a person this opportunity would give everyone in the school district a chance to evaluate the interim's leadership ability.

There are a number of advantages and some disadvantages to hiring from within. On the positive side, you are hiring someone who has proven ability in another position in the district. This person knows the people, problems, and challenges facing the schools. They will not need to take months to learn about the district. If the faculty, staff, and community are happy with what is going on in the district, an inside candidate can guarantee continuity and the maintenance of the current successful programs. A person who has already earned the respect of the school district is at a definite advantage as a new superintendent.

Of course, there are some potential problems with an internal appointment. The new superintendent must develop a different relationship with the rest of the administrative team. Instead of being one of many advisors to the superintendent, the new chief school officer will now have the last word. There will also be the need for this person to supervise and evaluate people who have been friends and peers. In this role, the superintendent will need to recommend pay raises and possibly disciplinary action for people to whom he or she has been very close. In addition, the new responsibility will require that a person think about what is best for the entire organization, rather than about a single school or program. A former assistant superintendent for business must become the instructional leader of the district as well, while an individual who served as a principal needs to think about public relations, budgets, and developing an appropriate relationship with the board of education. As the chief advisor to the board, the superintendent is ultimately responsible not to a superior in the organization but directly to the board. Instead of being evaluated by the superintendent for carrying out a specific responsibility in the district, the newly appointed chief school officer needs to quickly accept the fact that he or she is now responsible for everything that happens in the district and that continued employment will depend on maintaining the support of a majority of the members of the school board.

Many successful superintendents have made a successful transition from a lower level administrative position into the superintendency in their district. Still, if at the time of a vacancy there is not a person who appears to be an overwhelmingly popular choice within the district, a school board should initiate a search process.

A major decision that must be made at the outset of a search is whether a consultant should be hired to guide the board through the process. There will be need for help, especially if board members have never experienced a superintendent search process. It is possible that a chief school officer who is retiring or leaving the district can provide the necessary expertise. Consultants are often quite expensive and sometimes boards have questioned the value of their services. Still, unless there is someone in the district who can successfully guide the process, a board can make some serious errors. For instance, it is essential that the announcement of the position be well done and distributed to the appropriate sources to ensure that potential candidates are aware of the vacancy. It is also absolutely necessary that someone does very careful reference checks on all serious candidates. This may well include visits to the candidate's current school and community. In selecting a consultant, it may not be necessary to contract for the entire package of services offered. Consulting firms will offer to prepare "needs assessment studies," which might entail coming to the district and doing significant interviewing and meeting with groups. This is something that some boards have done for themselves. In any case, the choice of a new superintendent is so important to a district that most large and medium-size communities have chosen to use a consultant for some of the steps required in the selection process.

Since the search might take from six months to a year, it is often necessary to appoint an interim administrator during the process. In most states, there is a large pool of retired superintendents who move from district to district to fulfill this function. It is not unusual for these individuals to be paid up to $10,000 per month if they have a proven record as a "fill-in superintendent." Before interviewing any candidates for interim positions, it is important that boards check any candidate's references very carefully. Someone should talk personally to board members and employees where the candidate had worked. Sending out a standard reference form is seldom enough.

With an interim superintendent, the board is not necessarily seeking someone with great vision and creativity but rather an individual who can help to maintain a peaceful and positive environment in the district. The person should also have a proven record as an effective manager. Interim superintendents should not be expected to introduce sweeping changes in the district. There are a number of people, particularly retired superintendents, who have reached the point in their lives where they are considered wise "elder statesmen." Such an individual can often help to heal a divided district.

With an interim superintendent in place, the board can now begin to develop its plan for a search. Before a board proceeds to the first step of the process, the board should consider whether to look outside the traditional educational community for a superintendent. In many states, this is not an alternative because of certification requirements for administrators. In recent years, a number of districts have hired individuals from the business community or even former military leaders. Presently, three of the largest districts in the United States (New York, Los Angeles, and Chicago) have chief executive officers who have come from fields outside public education.[5]

Since the development of school districts, it has been assumed that a superintendent would first be a teacher. Most people believed that in order to be an instructional leader in a school district, the chief school officer should have at least spent some time as a classroom teacher. For some, an exception would be similar to having as managing partner in a law firm someone who had never studied or practiced law.

In recent years, especially in large districts, some boards of education have concluded that managing a large school system is not significantly different from managing a business or being a high-level officer in the military. Board members who support this position view the primary role of a superintendent of schools to be a motivator and a manager. Individuals with these skills can delegate the day-to-day curriculum and instructional issues to assistant superintendents and principals.

Others would argue that superintendents are more effective if they have previous experience as a teacher and as a principal. Serving as a building principal provides valuable experience working with unions, parents, and community groups. Even supporters of this idea admit that previous experience working as a building principal in a school does not in itself prepare someone to be a superintendent. The same can be said about working in a central office position. Assistant superintendents sometimes have little power to make independent decisions and it might even be argued that a building principal has more experience in making choices than anyone in the central office, with the sole exception of the superintendent. Because of the special training in school administration and the seeming importance of experience working in a school, most educators have been critical of the practice of bringing in an outsider to administer a school district. Even though this still represents the conventional wisdom, there have been examples where this practice has been successful.

John Stanford was a county executive and a retired major general before being selected as the superintendent of schools in Seattle. His work there was given national recognition in a Public Broadcasting System special report titled "Tale of Three Cities."[6] The program told the story of how the charismatic Stanford was able to work successfully with the employees' unions and the community to bring about constructive change in a large urban district. There were also a number of news stories that reported the reaction of Seattle's citizens when their superintendent became critically ill. This outpouring of sympathy and emotion demonstrates that someone in the position of superintendent of schools can be a major figure in the community. John Stanford's book, *Victory in Our Schools*, also won for him admiration throughout the country for his accomplishments in Seattle. The PBS radio program also highlighted the trials and tribulations of David Hornbeck, who was hired in 1994 to lead the Philadelphia school district. Hornbeck, a minister and a lawyer, antagonized the teachers of the city. According to the program, his tenure was characterized primarily by strife and gridlock. Other cities have looked outside education for their leadership. New

Orleans ... e colonel, while a former federal pros-

ecutor v ...

It is ... ate whether this hiring pattern will be-

come m ... mportant question is whether it will have

positive ... chools. In any case, it has been prima-

rily larg ... ave selected superintendents from out-

side the ... ty. Because these large organizations

have m ... hief school officer has available experts

in ever ... t business. For most school districts, it

would ... lect a superintendent who can be an in-

structic ... ws about teaching and learning.

After considering this option, the board can begin to develop a plan for finding the right superintendent for their district. There is no single best way to do this that is right for all districts, but there are some steps that all districts should consider.

1. The board needs to ask the question, who should be involved in the process? It is possible to establish separate committees made up of community members, faculty, nonteaching personnel, and possibly even students to participate in the process. A joint committee of all of these parties can also be formed. Any committee must be given a clear mission statement that outlines the role of the group. The questions that need to be considered when appointing any such group would include a decision as to whether the group should aid in forming the brochure or announcement advertising vacancy. Will the committee or committees help to screen the applications? Should the group participate in the interview process? If they are given this job, will they be responsible for choosing a number of finalists to be presented to the board of education? Perhaps most important when a district considers any type of involvement in the choice of the superintendent is making it clear to all participants that the final decision will be made by the board of education. If the committee does a preliminary screening, the board might be wise to merely ask them to name perhaps five finalists, but not request that these finalists be prioritized. When advisory committees are given the opportunity to select their first choice and the person is not chosen, it can create

hard feelings. Of course, a board can choose not to involve others in the selection process. Failure to do so might well result in criticism from faculty members and district administrators. In this age of "participatory democracy," there is an expectation among professionals in schools that they will be involved in major decisions. Once the decision on advisory committees has been made and the duties of such groups are carefully articulated and shared, the district is ready to proceed.

2. For many districts, the next step is a needs assessment. In preparing such a document, there must be a serious discussion of the strengths and weaknesses of the district. Questions dealing with faculty and staff morale, academic achievement, community support, and the financial condition of the district need to be discussed in detail. Such a dialogue will help the district move to the next step in the search process.

3. With the needs assessment in hand, it now becomes necessary to create a document outlining the profile of qualifications desired in the successful candidate. Is the greatest need for someone who can improve the business operation of the schools? Perhaps the needs assessment identifies problems with the academic program and what the district needs most is an effective instructional leader. Other districts might be seeking an excellent communicator who can gain the support of the public community for the schools. It could be that what is needed is a "peacemaker" to bring calm to a conflict-ridden school and community. The opposite is also possible in that some districts may be seeking a reformer to shake up the seeming stagnation inherent in their organization. Creating a written profile of what is needed in a person can also help in developing questions to ask the candidate's references, as well as questions to be used during the interview process. This profile should be an important guide in helping the board find the right person.

With the profile completed, it is now advisable to prepare a brochure announcing the vacancy. This publication should contain:

- a description of the district and community
- a description of "the person wanted"

- some indication of salary
- application procedures and processes[7]

This announcement of the vacancy should be professionally printed and distributed to the state superintendent's organization, major universities that prepare school administrators, and a wide range of school districts. Ads may be taken in a number of professional periodicals. As part of the pamphlet, an address should be given where candidates can gain additional information and a formal application. All interested candidates should be asked to send a completed application along with a current résumé. The application should include questions that will help the screening committee gain some knowledge about the responsibilities the candidate has had in previous positions, an understanding of the person's educational philosophy, as well as the individual's professional accomplishments. The application could also include leadership roles, professional presentations, and publications. Perhaps most important, there should be a place for the names, addresses, and telephone numbers of references. It is important that the reference section include a blank for listing the position held by the reference. In preparing to check references, it is helpful to list in advance questions to ask the individuals provided. These questions should relate directly to the position profile created by the district. Rather than have the personal references fill out a form, conversations in person or over the telephone offer the opportunity to make follow-up inquiries and perhaps to more effectively elicit possible weaknesses in a candidate. Many people are more willing to say something on a one-to-one basis rather than putting their thoughts in writing. This is especially true today when negative references can and do end up as lawsuits. As mentioned earlier, it is also very helpful to visit a candidate's current district to talk with people who have not been listed as references—perhaps individuals you might meet in a convenience store or at a local gas station. Whenever possible, it is helpful to talk to employees of the candidate's current district. If board members have friends or relatives in the community from which the candidate is moving or has served in the past, it is also possible to find something about the person's reputation in the district. Of course, past or present board members who have worked with the candidate provide an excellent source of information.

As the applications begin to arrive, the actual screening can begin. If a consultant has been engaged, that person will often do the screening and an initial check on references. Whoever does the paper screening should use the profile that has been prepared to identify those candidates who seem from their application material to be closest to the ideal.

Once a small number of candidates has been identified for an initial interview, those chosen can be notified and a mutually convenient time can be determined. Whether the screening or initial interviews are conducted by a committee or by one or two individuals, time should be taken to prepare a list of questions to be asked of each of the candidates. Again, the position profile should be a guide for the questions to be asked. It is also important for any candidate to learn as much as possible about the district during this visit. Those conducting the interview should not hide any problems that are currently present in the schools or in the community. Any potential chief school officer has a right to know in advance the difficulties that might lie ahead. It is possible that as many as ten candidates might be brought to the district for initial screening interviews. While a number of interviews can be done in one sitting, it is wise not to do more than three in one day. Although these discussions can be as informal as possible, it is not inappropriate to have prepared questions and a rating sheet for each candidate. Filling out the evaluation should wait until the candidate has left the room. Many screening committees like to leave a half hour after each interview to fill out the forms and briefly discuss the candidate.

Once these interviews are completed, those who have done the initial interviews should take as long as necessary to select the final candidates who will be interviewed by the board of education. Should the initial screening not yield at least three acceptable candidates, the group might wish to have some additional interviews. If the pool of candidates is weak, the district may wish to consider whether the position has been adequately advertised. The board members might also have to ask themselves whether the proposed salary is adequate. It is better to continue the search than to send to the board candidates about whom the screening committee is less than enthusiastic.

In the instructions to the group doing the screening, the board has either requested that the finalists be ranked or given to them without a listed priority. Again, it must be emphasized that the board of education might very well wish that the candidates not be ranked. The interviews with the board quite often are full-day affairs. During the day, the candidate will tour the facilities and meet with various groups, which could include administrators, faculty, staff, parents, and students. This can be followed by a late afternoon session with the board. In some cases, the board might wish to talk to the candidate informally during dinner and follow that with an evening interview. All of the groups meeting the final candidates can be asked to complete an evaluation form. In the past, it was not unusual to have the candidate's spouse participate during the visit. Frequently this included being a guest during dinner. Most districts will pay the expenses of the final candidates, including overnight accommodations for those who traveled a long distance.

If it is possible, the final interviews should be scheduled in a relatively short period of time. It is essential, even if the board is especially impressed by one of the first candidates interviewed, that everyone maintain an open mind until the final candidate has visited the district.

As a board prepares for the final interview, it is helpful to carefully consider the personal characteristics that define a successful leader. One quality that appears to be necessary for a successful superintendent is what many have labeled as vision. An individual who seeks to be a successful superintendent must have some convictions as to what is essential for an excellent school district. A leader who lacks a conception of excellence will not lead but rather will be blown about by the winds of change. A good question to test a candidate's vision is to ask the person to describe the ideal school district.

A conception of the ideal in itself is not enough to ensure the success of a chief school officer. The individual must also possess the political skills to bring about positive change in the district. Even the notion of political skills creates a negative connotation for many Americans. Webster defines politics as "the science of government."[8] Superintendents are involved in the process of governance and, as a result, they do need some specific political skills. These include the ability to communicate effectively when speaking to large or small groups, and in a one-on-one setting. The superintendent must also be an effective writer. It is necessary to have the ability to bring about a consensus within a group and on occasion be able to compromise on one's own preferences.

As a leader, it is essential to be an excellent judge of potential personnel for the district. No superintendent can survive who does not have the ability to select effective people for the key positions in the district.

Once hired, the chief school officer must earn and maintain the respect of the faculty, staff, and community. This can only be done if the leader is a person of unquestionable integrity. One who is perceived as being personally honest is much more likely to gain the trust of others. These qualities of leadership are difficult to identify in a job candidate.

There are several ways to attempt to judge a candidate's political skills and integrity. One possible method to be used in the interview process is to provide a number of situation simulations that would give to the person a set of possible problems requiring the candidate to develop a plan to resolve a particular administrative dilemma. The simulations can also force the candidate to make ethical decisions. If a candidate in an interview makes an expedient choice of tactics over a more ethical approach, it will be quite easy to determine how this person might react in actual political situations. Examples of this type of simulation are contained in a number of case study books, which could be made available to board members.[9]

Finally, it is important to judge the candidate as a human being. Is this a person who enjoys other people, especially children? Can this person laugh at himself or herself, as well as enjoy a laugh with others? It is admirable to be totally committed to one's job but it is healthier to be a person who enjoys life and truly cares for other people. These characteristics are difficult to judge; potential employers must remember they are not selecting a machine but rather a person who can gain the respect and affection of a community. Candidates can be very impressive during visits but react differently when they assume the position. This is another reason to investigate the candidate's background very carefully. The board cannot afford to find out six months later that their new superintendent has a criminal record or was about to be fired from a previous position.

After completing the interviews and doing exhaustive reference checks, the board is ready to make a decision. Hopefully, a consensus will emerge quickly. The person chosen might not be everyone's first choice, but the entire board must be comfortable with the selection. A new superintendent will be starting with a great disadvantage if his or her appointment is the result of a four-to-three vote of a divided board. If there is significant opposition to the choice of the majority, it might well be best to reopen the search. In any case, the public motion making the formal appointment should, if possible, occur with a unanimous vote of the board.

Once a decision has been made, the president of the board should contact the individual chosen and arrangements should be made to meet in order to discuss the terms of a contract. The school attorney should be consulted in advance when preparing the contract for a new superintendent. It might well be that the attorney would be assigned to work with the new chief school officer to develop a contract. The board should agree on the following issues prior to a meeting with the person chosen to lead the district:

- length of contract (frequently, a superintendent's contract will run from one to three years)
- salary
- fringe benefits (paid holidays, vacation days, health insurance, pension benefits)
- professional budget (to be used for travel expenses and attendance at professional conferences)
- provisions for dealing with the process for renewal or nonrenewal of the superintendent's contract
- the procedure for evaluating the superintendent's performance

Once a contract is agreed upon, an announcement should be given first to the employees and then to the media. Every effort should be made to portray the new chief school officer in a positive light. When the new superintendent arrives in the district to assume the position, the board might consider sponsoring a public reception. During the early days of the new superintendency, it is important that board members demonstrate their enthusiasm for the appointment and their support of the new superintendent.

Once installed, the challenge for both the superintendent and the board is to create a relationship that forges a strong partnership. The importance of this relationship is the subject of the next chapter.

NOTES

1. Herb Cottril, National School Boards Association News Service, "Superintendent Shortage May Be Reaching Crisis Stages," *Virginia School Boards Association Newsletter* April 2000, www.vsba.org (13 December 2000).

2. Cottril, "Superintendent Shortage."

3. AASA Online, "Superintendents: Who Will Fill Their Shoes?" *AASA Online*, www.aasa.org/Issues/Women/shepard1-13-99.htm (26 October 2000).

4. National School Boards Association, "Solutions to Superintendent Crisis Proposed," *National School Boards Association* 12 September 2000, http://www.nsba.org/sbn/00-sep/091200-6.htm (21 September 2000).

5. National School Boards Association, "Non-educator Named in Philly," *School Board News* 24 October 2000, www.nsba.org/sbn (2 November 2000).

6. *The Merrill Report*, 1999.

7. Illinois Association of School Boards, "Information for School Boards Seeking Superintendents," *Illinois Association of School Boards*, www.iasb. com/files/infosb.htm (9 October 2000).

8. *Webster's New World Dictionary* (New York: Macmillan Company, 1959), 577.

9. William Hayes, *Real-Life Case Studies for School Administrators* (Lanham, Md.: Scarecrow Press, 2000).

CHAPTER 6

The Relationship between Board Members and the Superintendent

Currently, the average tenure of superintendents in urban communities is approximately two and a half years. Suburban school leaders now stay in a district from five to six years.[1] One of the major factors causing this high turnover rate is the failure of the relationship between boards of education and their chief school officers.

Perhaps the most difficult aspect of this relationship is establishing a fairly clear-cut understanding and agreement as to the appropriate roles for the superintendent and the board. Board members need to remember that a school board is a public corporate body. In this sense, it could be compared to a board of directors of a local bank or the Ford Motor Company. The board of education appoints the superintendent as the chief executive officer of the organization. A single board member has no legal standing. As a corporate body, it must act as a committee of the whole. In dealing with any issue, board members have the obligation to question, suggest, and participate in debates, but at the end of the discussion, it is the action approved by the majority that prevails. Once a resolution has passed, it then becomes the responsibility of the chief school officer to carry it out. This comparison is not a perfect one. Corporate board members are responsible to the stockholders while school board members are elected representatives of the people. Even though they are democratically elected, board members have no powers that they can exercise as individuals.

It is frequently suggested that it is the job of the board of education to make policy and the role of the superintendent to carry out that policy. Unfortunately, this division of powers is easier to articulate than to implement. In all school districts, the development of policy is a joint responsibility. As a professional educator and manager, the superintendent is expected to recommend policy. Problems often occur when superintendents become too independent in the practice of developing district policy. There have always been superintendents who become uncomfortable when board members ask hard questions or disagree with their recommendations. Chief school officers who seem to resent board member input during policy discussions can be perceived as being overly sensitive and dogmatic. In such situations, boards begin to feel that their superintendent is merely looking for quick approval of all recommendations. When a chief school officer creates this type of impression, it can cause the board to conclude that the superintendent expects them to be a "rubber stamp" for administrative proposals.

On the other hand, there are many board of education members who seek to become involved in issues that are clearly administrative. Board members must ensure that there are policies and procedures for the selection of instructional materials but they do not have the personal responsibility to choose textbooks. If the varsity basketball coach is not using his players in a way that satisfies a board member, this does not need to be a public discussion at a board meeting. Most superintendents are extremely sensitive about what they might consider "micromanaging" by board members. Superintendents often leave a district or are fired because of conflict that arises over the proper division of roles between them and their board of education.

How can such a problem best be avoided? A wise superintendent will quickly make an effort to get to know individual board members. As noted earlier, the superintendent should take the time to give a thorough orientation to all new board members. Attending meetings together and even an occasional social event can enhance a personal relationship. Along with getting to know each other in a context outside of meetings, there are also several simple rules that will help to avoid unnecessary conflict.

First of all, when a new superintendent is hired, the board president should share with the new administrator how the board has functioned in the past. Prior to making changes, there should be a frank discussion about several issues. For instance, the question of how agendas are developed should be reviewed and made clear to all board members. Ideally, the superintendent will prepare the agendas, perhaps in consultation with the board president. All board members must have the opportunity to have an item placed on the agenda as long as it is submitted prior to a predetermined deadline.

Once the agenda has been published, nothing should be added except for emergency items. When unexpected issues are placed on the agenda, neither the board members nor the superintendent should feel obligated to respond publicly without first having time to investigate the matter. Even when the public is allowed to speak at meetings and unexpected issues are raised, it is not inappropriate to announce that it will be necessary to look into the question before giving a definitive response. If the issue raised is a sensitive personnel item or relates to labor negotiations, the board should discuss it in executive session before responding publicly. The most important understanding regarding meetings is that neither the superintendent nor the board should be surprised by a topic that is raised. As it is not fair for a superintendent to seek from the board a decision without providing in advance the necessary data upon which to base a judgment, it is equally disturbing when board members embarrass a superintendent by raising unexpected issues in a public meeting. Surprises of this sort by either party erode the level of trust that is necessary for a positive relationship. The procedure for preparing and adding to agendas should be clearly understood by the entire management team and would need to be reviewed at the beginning of a new superintendent's career in the district.

It should also be understood that it is the responsibility of the administration to provide complete backup data on all agenda items. This material should be sent to all board members at least three days before the meeting. This backup packet should include information about all of those being recommended for employment in the district. There should be written background on any major issues upon which the board is expected to make a decision. The superintendent should not wait until the meeting to give board members handouts that they do not have a chance to read thoroughly before being expected to take action. At the same time, a conscientious board member should study the material carefully. It is very discouraging for a superintendent when a board member opens the packet publicly at the beginning of a meeting. Equally disconcerting is when board members continually ask questions that are clearly answered in the material that had been sent to them.

Another understanding that should be reached at the outset of a new superintendency is the development of a procedure for board members to deal with concerns expressed to them by citizens or staff members. Most superintendents will ask that board members call the superintendent directly when they have received some sort of complaint. Board members should be asked to be noncommittal when receiving a complaint until the superintendent or another administrator has an opportunity to investigate the issue. Following the investigation, either the board member or a member of the administration needs to respond to the person's concerns. Such issues should not be thrust upon a superintendent by a board member at a public meeting. There will be concerns expressed to board members and the best procedure is for these problems to be dealt with primarily by the administration.

Developing a team approach to leading and managing the school district must be the primary goal of both the superintendent and the board of education. One of the best ways to ensure such a partnership is to develop clear objectives for the district. Although it is very time consuming, every district needs to have a limited number of long-term goals that will result in some measurable annual objectives. If a district has a goal of raising the reading levels of all students, an objective for a particular year might be to raise the reading scores in grades one through three by 5 percent. A goal that seeks to increase offerings for gifted and talented students might establish an objective for the coming year of creating three advanced placement courses.

With these yearly objectives in place, the district then has a focus for their work during the coming year. To be most effective, district objectives should not come via a "top-down" announcement. It is more appropriate that the goals and objectives are the result of a districtwide discussion that identifies the primary needs of the school system. The value of the process of creating these targets will be seen in several ways. Once a district has a clear-cut direction for its efforts, the resulting objectives will be helpful in both budget and personnel decisions. If raising reading scores is the objective, money should be earmarked for specific staff development in reading, for additional teachers or aides, or perhaps for enriched classroom libraries. Having agreed-upon priorities will help stimulate the efforts of both the superintendent and the board to work for a common purpose.

These same objectives can also be utilized in the evaluation instrument used for the superintendent and the board. To avoid misunderstandings and to ensure ongoing communication, a superintendent should be evaluated annually. The format of this evaluation process should be jointly agreed upon. Perhaps the best approach is to ask the superintendent to provide a draft of a form that could be modified and approved by the board. Help in establishing an effective procedure for evaluation is available from most state school board associations or superintendents' organizations. In any case, the evaluation should in part be tied to the district's objectives. Both the superintendent and the board should be held accountable each year for the progress, or lack of progress, in meeting the mutually agreed-upon goals.

The annual evaluation of the superintendent should be a time when using an agreed-upon format, the performance of the superintendent can be honestly discussed. Such discussions should not wait until the end of the year. A midyear conversation, using the evaluation form as a format, can be very helpful. Potential problems can be identified and dealt with before they become too serious. If the superintendent is behaving in a way that is disturbing to one or more board members, someone should share this information with the chief school officer. Most often, the individual to deal with the potential problems is the president of the board. It is not unusual for the president to act as an intermediary between the superintendent and board members. An ideal relationship between a board president and a superintendent would be characterized by mutual respect and trust. If these two individuals can learn to communicate regularly and honestly, many possible problems can be avoided. Just as the superintendent should be reviewed annually, a board might consider a self-evaluation each year and perhaps give the superintendent the opportunity to share his or her impression as to how the board is functioning.

Another potential difficulty with the relationship between a board of education and a superintendent occurs when the chief school officer seems to have favorites on the board. A wise superintendent will make every effort to treat board members equally. If Christmas cards are sent to one board member, they should be sent to all. Information must be shared equally with all board members. The social relationship between individual board members and the superintendent is also a sensitive area. Board members must always remember that they will have to evaluate the superintendent. Collectively, as a board, they are the chief school officer's employer. A close friendship between a board member and the superintendent can lead to a feeling among board members that the superintendent is showing favoritism. This is not to say that board members should not socialize with the superintendent outside of the boardroom, but rather that personal relationships can, and do, affect the way board members think of each other. No board member wants to be considered by others to be in the superintendent's "hip pocket" because of a personal friendship.

There are several other ways to help maintain a positive working relationship between the superintendent and the board of education. The tone of the discussions during public meetings and in private needs to be professional. Even when there are disagreements, everyone must avoid sarcasm and anger. If people can be polite and truly listen to each other, trust and respect will develop. Individual board members can contribute to a good working climate by avoiding outbursts, name-calling, and unjustified stubbornness. Nothing is more stressful to a superintendent than working in an atmosphere in which people treat each other poorly. Boards of education who can laugh together and enjoy each other's company are more likely to hold onto an excellent superintendent than a group that is constantly bickering and cannot work together.

It also helps any relationship when board members regularly recognize contributions that have been made to the district. The superintendent, along with other employees, deserves appropriate commendations from the board. As a school and community leader, any chief school officer receives both public and private criticism. Compliments from any quarter are infrequent. A public thank-you to a superintendent for a job well done would be greatly appreciated. There will also be times when board members may be called upon to defend an action taken by the superintendent. A chief school officer's job is often a lonely one and the support of the board of education can be very comforting. Even the most self-confident superintendent can occasionally feel uneasy when they reflect on the fact that four members of the seven-member board of education can decide at any time that their employment in the district should be terminated. The board of education is in a position to either make their chief school officer feel supported and appreciated, or insecure and discouraged.

There will be times when the relationship between a board and the superintendent just are not right and efforts to work together prove to be unsuccessful. When it becomes evident that a superintendent's tenure in the district must be ended, the board must do so in a way that is both sensitive and legal. Most superintendents' contracts contain specific language concerning contract renewal and dismissal. To avoid public controversy and possible legal action against the district, a board must be aware of the specific language in the contract and be sure that it is followed carefully. Before taking any action on a superintendent's future employment, a board would be wise to involve the school attorney in order to ensure that the action is taken in a legal manner. Frequently, there are dates that serve as deadlines for notifying the superintendent of the board's intentions. If a district does not follow these guidelines exactly, their actions could later be ruled invalid.

Rather than have the district go through a public controversy over the renewal of a superintendent's contract, giving a chief school officer the opportunity to resign can avoid a good deal of unpleasantness. If this option is offered, it must be done in a way that the administrator has ample opportunity to find a new position. A resignation will in most cases give the person a better chance to find a new position and save the superintendent's family public embarrassment. Sometimes a board wishes to make a change before the expiration of the chief school officer's contract. The procedure in such a situation often entails "buying out" the remainder of the contract. If a superintendent has a year left on the contract, the board could agree to pay the person's salary for that final year. In negotiating a buyout, boards of education certainly should involve the school district attorney.

Although turnover remains a major problem, there are a number of districts that have been successful in keeping outstanding superintendents. The continuity, peace, and progress that are often evident in such districts make it beneficial for school boards and superintendents to work together to create a team that will ensure the highest possible level of academic achievement for the children of the district.

NOTE

1. Peter J. Negroni, "The Right Badge of Courage," *AASA Online*, February 1999, www.aasa.org/SA/feb9904.htm (26 October 2000).

CHAPTER 7

Board Relationships
with Other School Employees

Although school boards work most closely with superintendents and other administrators, it is also essential that the elected representatives of the district develop a positive relationship with all employee groups. Of all of the district employees, the faculty is the largest and most influential. Until the rise of the teacher union movement almost a half century ago, superintendents and boards of education had almost absolute power over most local educational decisions made in the district. Teachers were not active in affecting either curriculum or their own levels of compensation. Hiring and evaluating teachers was the sole responsibility of the administration and the board. As we enter a new century, teacher unions have become extremely influential in most school districts. The paternalistic approach to school governance has become a thing of the past. Too often, as faculty members have become part of decision making, the relationship between teachers and the board has become antagonistic. A number of boards see the teacher unions, if not teachers themselves, as "the enemy." It is also true that some teachers see the board as a major obstacle to their own personal and professional aspirations.

This type of relationship is extremely unhealthy for a school district. Both boards of education and teacher unions should be seeking ways to cooperate for the good of the children. There appears to be a healthy change of attitude in the upper echelon of leadership in the National Education Association and the American Federation of Teachers. There has been a good deal of rhetoric recently about the need to calm the adversarial relationship that has grown in many districts. Bob Chase, president of the National Education Association, talked about the challenges facing public education in a speech before the National Press Club in 1997. He said the following:

> Bear in mind that, for nearly three decades now, the National Education Association has been a traditional, somewhat narrowly focused union. We have butted heads with management over bread-and-butter issues — to win better salaries, benefits, and working conditions for school employees. And we have succeeded.
>
> Today, however, it is clear to me — and to a critical mass of teachers across America — that while this narrow, traditional agenda remains important, it is utterly inadequate to the needs of the future. It will not serve our members' interest in greater professionalism. It will not serve the public's interest in better quality public schools. And it will not serve the interests of America's children . . . the children we teach . . . the children who motivated us to go into teaching in the first place.
>
> And this latter interest must be decisive. After all, America's public schools do not exist for teachers and other employees. They do not exist to provide us with jobs and salaries. Schools do exist for the children — to give the students the very best . . . beginning with a quality teacher in every classroom.
>
> Ladies and gentlemen, the imperative now facing public education could not be more stark: Simply put, in the decade ahead, we must revitalize our public schools from within, or they will be dismantled from without. And I am not talking here about the critics on talk radio who seek higher ratings by bashing public education and trashing teachers. I am talking about the vast majority of Americans who support public education, but are clearly dissatisfied. They want higher quality public schools, and they want them now.[1]

As union leadership and boards of education realize that it is in everyone's best interest to cooperate, it is very likely that in the next decade we may together be able to improve our public schools. It is also true that the economic prosperity in recent years has quieted some of the labor strife in many states. As a result, it would seem an excellent time for boards of education to begin a constructive dialogue with their faculties. This is especially true because in the next decade we will see large numbers of new teachers coming into our schools. "An enrollment boom, mandated class-size reductions, more full-day kindergarten and prekindergarten classes, and a surge of retirees," have all contributed to a current teacher shortage.[2] The United States Education Department has estimated that in the United States we will require 2.2 million new faculty members by 2010.

Many districts are struggling to find enough qualified teachers to fill their classrooms. The shortage has been recognized in Congress, where Senator Charles Schumer has introduced legislation that would encourage people to enter the teaching profession. His proposal, called a "Marshall Plan" for teachers, would offer a $20,000 scholarship for college students who would agree at graduation to teach in "high-need urban and rural areas."[3]

Signing bonuses for new teachers have also become more prevalent. Even in high-paying states like Massachusetts, the legislature has sought to encourage teacher education students to take jobs within the state. In 1999, legislation was passed that offered an additional $20,000 to a teacher who would commit to teaching four years in the state. The competition for outstanding teachers is greatest in fields like math and science. Districts are often now actively recruiting teachers from neighboring schools. This is especially true of suburban districts whose higher salaries are extremely attractive to those teaching in cities or rural areas.

In the recent past, the supply of teachers has been more than ample. Suburban schools have often had hundreds of applicants for elementary and social studies vacancies. Although this may still be true in some affluent areas, rural and urban districts in many states are having problems filling their classrooms with qualified instructors. Districts are sending out representatives to college campuses and job fairs. Advertising positions has spread to the local newspaper and other periodicals. Competition is especially spirited for those communities that are seeking to increase the number of minority teachers.

Some districts are dealing with the problem by hiring primarily local individuals or those who have substituted in the district. These candidates should of course always be given the opportunity to apply, but a school district cannot ignore its responsibility to find the very best possible candidates. This may well mean that boards of education need to spend additional money to send administrators on recruiting trips.

Finding enough good teachers is only part of the challenge. In an article in *Education Update*, published by the Association for Supervision and Curriculum Development, Lynn Nordgren, facilitator of the Professional Development Process in the Minneapolis Public Schools, is quoted as saying "we know that nationwide we lose half of all new teachers during the first five years of teaching."[4] One of the major reasons that teachers leave the profession is the lack of support they feel during their initial teaching experience. Survival is the primary objective of most first teachers. It has become clear that one way to help new teachers is to provide them with a seasoned mentor during their first several years in the profession. There have always been veteran teachers in every school who have taken it upon themselves to offer help to new faculty members. Unfortunately, too many new teachers are not being given this type of guidance. Still others are too proud or insecure to seek assistance. Many districts have instituted a formalized program for mentoring new faculty members. Peer assistance has also proven extremely helpful for experienced teachers who are facing problems.

This need has recently been recognized in California, where teacher unions and the state school board association created a program that resulted in innovative law. Money is now available in California for districts to provide $5680 to teachers who act as mentors. A district plan that is approved can create mentor positions for up to 5 percent of its faculty. These mentors work with new teachers and also must be available as consultants for veteran teachers who have received "unsatisfactory evaluations or those who voluntarily seek help."[5]

Other states have also made available limited funds for teacher-mentor programs, but in most cases, individual districts have taken the initiative to begin their own local program. If this is done, it should be done jointly with the district's faculty union. One way to achieve a satisfactory plan is to create a task force that includes teachers appointed by the union, administrators, and possibly even a board member. When creating a teacher-mentor program, the board must be very sensitive to the role of the building principal. As the district administrator who has the primary responsibility for assisting and evaluating teachers, it is essential that building principals be included in the planning process. It is also true that the amount of money to be used to implement such a program may have to be negotiated as part of the teacher contract. However it is done, a mentor program should have the support of the union and the district administrators. Relying on the hope that experienced teachers will automatically provide help that new teachers need is wishful thinking. In addition, it is quite unlikely that busy building administrators will be able to meet the needs of all of the new teachers who are entering our schools. Mentoring will not be effective for all new teachers. "Beginning teachers can display widely different attitudes toward the help offered by a mentor. One year, a mentor may work with a beginning teacher hungry for advice and the next year be assigned a beginning teacher who reacts defensively to thoughtfully offered suggestions."[6]

Those teachers selected as mentors must be carefully prepared for their new role. Any plan must clearly define the expectations for mentors and provide ongoing staff development opportunities. In the UCLA Laboratory Elementary School, each mentor, or teacher-leader, is given one day of release time each week to carry out the following functions:

- meet with the principal to discuss progress and set new goals
- visit classrooms to observe other teachers and gain a schoolwide perspective on curriculum
- assist other teachers in improving their practices by planning with them, demonstrating lessons, providing feedback on observed lessons, sharing assessment strategies, and providing resources
- enhance his or her own knowledge of subject matter and of effective practices by attending conferences, reading, or consulting with outside experts, and
- help the school develop a coherent instructional program with clear, well-articulated standards.[7]

Empowering master teachers to help new members of the profession is just one way to retain talented faculty members who might otherwise become discouraged.

An ongoing program of staff development for all teachers is an extremely helpful way to make teachers more effective and more fulfilled in their profession. Congress has established a procedure for teachers anyplace in the United States to gain national certification. A recent survey has shown that "teachers who are certified by a National Standards Board outperform other teachers on almost all measures of teaching expertise."[8] For instance, the research showed "that 74 percent of the work samples collected from students taught by board-certified teachers reflected a high level of intellectual comprehension, compared to 29 percent for students taught by teachers without the distinction."[9]

One individual who has been through the extended process of certification by the National Board for Professional Teaching Standards has written that "it doesn't come easy, but the rigorous experience may be the most powerful professional development of a teacher's career."[10] Because achieving national certification is a costly and time-consuming task for individual teachers, some districts are helping teachers pay for the process. Other school systems are giving salary increases to those who have achieved the goal of national certification.

National board certification and mentor programs are only a part of an ongoing faculty development process. Every true profession requires that practitioners remain active learners. A wise board of education helps and encourages an ongoing staff-development program. In the past, this sometimes meant allowing teachers to attend two or three teacher conferences each year. Often, these meetings consisted of an inspirational speaker or smorgasbord of unrelated topics. These meetings usually had little or no follow-up and the result was that the impact on the educational program was minimal. Districts have also spent large amounts of money to encourage teachers to take graduate courses that were only marginally related to their work in the classroom.

Increasingly, school districts are attempting to offer their teachers meaningful learning opportunities that will make a difference in their teaching. Table 7.1 shows one model for a successful staff development program.

It is not the role of a school board to decide on the specific staff development opportunities for the faculty. This is a task that should be performed by the administration in cooperation with the teaching staff. Still, the district must provide money for these programs and, like any

Table 7.1   A Template for Staff Development

- Step 1: Identify the purpose and the objectives of the meeting.
  What do you want participants to learn and be able to do as a result of this activity?
  Remember that the scope of the objective needs to fit the time allocated for the meeting.
- Step 2: Select the resource(s) you plan to use as a basis for the activity.
  Content: Journal articles, books, videos, inquiry kits
  Process: Overhead transparencies, flip chart, and so on
- Step 3: Prepare an agenda that fits the time frame available.
  Each agenda should include these elements.
    An Activator: An activity to elicit prior knowledge, beliefs, or attitudes
    Brief Input: Information drawn from the resources identified above and delivered by using multiple modalities (visual, auditory, or kinesthetic)
    Discussion: Opportunities for participants to reflect on and respond to the input
    Activities: Model brain-compatible learning activities
    A Summarizer: An activity to elicit reflection on content and process
    Next Steps: Personal commitments to follow up with a new strategy or action research.
- Step 4: Revisit or follow-up activities.
  Support strategies for teachers:
    Peer planning
    Peer teaching
    Peer coaching[1]

1. Patricia V. Magestro and Nancy Stanford-Blair, "A Tool for Meaningful Staff Development," *Educational Leadership* 57, no. 8 (May 2000): 31.

other expenditure, board members have the right to know how the funds are being spent. The following questions need to be asked:

1. Are the district's staff development offerings being used to further the agreed-upon objectives of the district?
2. Will these programs have a positive impact on student learning?
3. Is adequate provision being made for follow-up activities in order to ensure the implementation of the topics introduced during the preliminary sessions? (This has been a major weakness in many staff development plans.)

Even though faculty and staff development programs can and do have a positive impact, many states and local districts have not given them a high priority. When funds are limited, some districts feel that this area can be cut. This is done even though American businesses have learned that spending money on the continuing education of their employees is a good investment.

Whenever there is a discussion on how to improve the quality of instruction in our schools, the issue of teachers' salaries is almost always mentioned. Historically, our method for compensating teachers has usually been based on years of experience. A typical salary schedule today might start at $28,000 for the first year and after fifteen to twenty years, a teacher would reach the point where he or she might be paid $55,000 to $60,000 per year. For every year of experience, a faculty member would have received an automatic increment until the maximum had been reached. Of course, the schedule itself would be increased each time a new contract was signed. Most often, those who had reached the highest level on the schedule would also be given an increase with each new contract. In addition, many contracts call for extra amounts of money for teachers who have completed graduate work. This is especially true of those who might have achieved a master's degree.

There have been many attempts through the years to find alternatives to automatic pay increases. Career ladder plans are used in several states. Such a plan is based on the college model that requires faculty members to be promoted through a series of job titles in order to receive the maximum level of compensation. In colleges, teachers are instructors, assistant professors, associate professors, or full professors. Promotions are based on such considerations as teaching ability, research, publications, and service to the college and community. In public schools, the job titles would vary from district to district. Career ladders for teachers would also have different qualifications or reasons for promotion. The goal of such plans is to provide motivation for faculty members to meet certain desired professional objectives in order to earn additional money and prestige.

Merit pay has the same objective, but as noted earlier, it is not universally accepted by many teachers. Lynn M. Cornett has written that

> serious philosophical differences probably doomed merit pay programs from the start. For example, would large groups of teachers ever accept the programs when only 20 or 30 percent were likely to be rewarded in such a system? In a South Carolina survey, half of the teachers queried thought they were in the top 10 percent of teachers in the state.[11]

Still, efforts to establish merit plans continue. The school board in Cincinnati, Ohio, adopted a plan that abolished the district seniority-based schedule. The plan was developed jointly with the "Cincinnati Federation of Teachers." It calls for principals and master teachers to evaluate teachers every five years. Based on these reviews, faculty members will be placed in one of five categories. Each category will have an assigned salary. Those teachers in the lowest level would be paid $30,000 per year, while those in the highest category would be paid $62,500 per year.[12] Even with the occasional experiments, like the one in Cincinnati, opposition to merit pay for teachers is still strong. In an article in the *American School Board Journal*, "Merit Pay Won't Work," Richard Rothstein quarrels with the notion that merit pay helps to promote success in the corporate sector by pointing out that "a survey of business compensation experts reveals that, when quality of work is important, corporations do not generally evaluate professional employees by quantifiable goals, such as test scores. And private sector pay-for-performance plans more frequently use team incentives, not individual ones."[13] The same author concludes his article with this argument:

Opponents of merit pay rightly argue that teacher compensation cannot rest significantly on students' test scores, because teachers have only partial influence over how well students perform on standardized tests, and because individual merit pay plans defeat the teacher collaboration that education reform aims to encourage. But few critics of merit pay realize that the private sector long ago discovered a similar lesson. Some private firms use group rewards, but here, too, they are rarely based primarily on quantifiable measures. In the private sector, merit pay for professional employees typically requires qualitative evaluations supported by a supervisory structure far more intense than public schools can afford.[14]

There are other ways to alter the traditional method of compensating teachers. Extra pay for accomplishments such as national board certification has been endorsed by Sandra Feldman, president of the American Federation of Teachers. The number of teachers who are receiving this distinction is growing rapidly. California now offers a $10,000 bonus upon certification and North Carolina compensates teachers for the application fee and gives state aid for salary increases for nationally certified faculty members. There are a growing number of individuals at all levels in education who agree with Sandra Feldman when she writes that "national certification is a clear standard of teaching excellence."[15]

With 42 percent of all teachers now covered by contracts that allow additional compensation for national certification, more and more school districts are finding that this is an effective way to offer an opportunity for their teachers to achieve increased proficiency and higher status.[16]

Another approach is to reward teachers for specific knowledge and skills. There are now nationally recognized tests that assess a teacher's knowledge of content and effective pedagogical practices. These tests give districts an opportunity to assign pay increases to teachers as they increase their professional knowledge and skills.[17] At a time when only 38 percent of all teachers have an undergraduate major in an academic field, initiatives to increase a teacher's knowledge base seem appropriate. It is difficult to disagree with Dennis Sparks when he wrote in the *Harvard Education Letter* that

> the public needs to support quality staff development. Efforts to expand teachers' knowledge and skills will pay off for students if staff development is tied to clear and high standards for student learning and if every teacher is given ample time to learn, absorb, and implement the new techniques and technologies. Only then can we create a teaching force that is prepared to teach in tomorrow's classrooms.[18]

Finding an appropriate way to compensate teachers is only one of the issues that can cause conflict between faculty unions and boards of education. For decades, one of the most controversial issues in public schools has been teacher tenure. These laws were passed to assure the academic freedom of teachers and protect them from boards of education that too often dismissed faculty members for unfair reasons. In every state, there have been attempts to abolish or reform teacher tenure legislation. The current laws frequently make it extremely difficult and time consuming to discipline or remove an incompetent teacher. It can also be very expensive. As a result, school administrators hesitate to bring charges against unsatisfactory faculty members. Although tenure laws have been modified in some states, teacher unions usually oppose any major revisions in the statutes. As individual board members and as a member of your state school board association, a board member who feels strongly about the issue can support legislative efforts to amend the tenure laws.

For a more immediate response to the problem of poor teaching, there are several steps a board should consider. Every district should have in place a procedure for supervision and evaluation of probationary teachers. Such a system should offer as much help as possible to new teachers, but only those faculty members who have demonstrated true professional competence should be considered for tenure. Board members should insist that the administration carefully document the problems of probationary teachers and be prepared to defend tenure recommendations that are brought to the board. When a board member becomes aware of possible problems in the classroom of a probationary teacher, this information should be promptly shared with the administration.

There are examples in most schools of teachers who were quite impressive during their probationary period but later became less and less effective. Too often, busy administrators concentrate so heavily on probationary teachers that veteran teachers have little or no supervision or evaluation. This is not usually as true for employees in other public and private fields. Despite a popular misconception, most supervisors of teachers have a very heavy load as compared to middle managers in most businesses or government agencies. It is essential that a school district have enough supervisors to carry out an ongoing program of evaluation and supervision for both probationary and tenured teachers. Preventing "teacher burnout" also requires an ongoing staff development program. Despite a district's best efforts, it will occasionally be necessary to discipline or dismiss a teacher. Often, this will mean that the district will need to spend whatever is necessary to carry out this unpleasant task. Failing to act is unfair to the children of the community.

If a school system has had an effective evaluation program and has documented evidence, incompetent teachers can sometimes be convinced to voluntarily resign. If a teacher chooses not to submit a resignation, it can be expected that the faculty union will provide legal assistance for any hearing. This will require that the school district also engage an effective attorney. The state school board association can probably provide the names of attorneys who have experience in this type of legal proceeding.

There will be other times when outside legal expertise will be needed in dealing with teacher unions. The most likely time for conflict will be when negotiating a new contract with the faculty union. In approaching contract discussions with the teacher organization, a board of education must do its homework. Together with the administration, the board should carefully review the current contract. Building principals and other administrators should identify those provisions of the present contract that have caused grievances or other problems. Discussions should also be held to determine specific sections of the contract that should be amended and, at the same time, consideration should be given to new management prerogatives that might be proposed. In negotiations, it is often effective to not just defend against unwanted teacher amendments to the contract but rather to be proactive with some well-designed district initiatives. At the very least, these items can be dropped as "trade-offs" in exchange for union proposals that the district finds unacceptable. In addition, serious conversation needs to take place on the compensation package that will be offered to the union. These discussions must include an analysis of the impact of the proposed salary increases on future budgets. Along with considering the recent history of the consumer price index, board members should ask for information about teacher compensation in other local districts. Special attention needs to be paid to the starting salary because it must be kept competitive to entice new teachers to accept employment in the district. A close eye must also be kept on recent contract settlements within the region. After a consensus is reached among the board and the administration, a proposal or a "package" should be given to the teacher negotiating team at the first session. This comprehensive document should include all of the desired changes in the current contract, as well as an opening offer on salary. The board should expect that the teachers have also developed their own set of proposals. It needs to be understood by both sides that neither the board nor the faculty union will achieve all of their objectives during the negotiations.

Given the nature of negotiations, a number of compromises will be necessary. With this in mind, the board must establish for its negotiating team an upper limit on what would be an acceptable financial settlement. The team should also be aware of those issues that the board feels are nonnegotiable.

Another issue that must be determined prior to negotiations is the makeup of the district's negotiating team. A number of options can be considered. One or more members of the administration can be part of the team. In large districts where there are specially trained personnel officers, this individual can be assigned the role of chief negotiator. During formal negotiations, this person is the individual who will do most, if not all, of the talking at the table. Many districts hire a specialized attorney or labor relations expert to be their chief negotiator. One advantage of an outsider in this role is that the employee union can focus their frustration and anger on the outside spokesperson rather than administrators or board members. The fact that many teachers' groups use professional negotiators at the table has caused numerous boards to conclude that they too need a paid professional. The obvious disadvantages for the district are that the contract talks can become very impersonal and expensive. It is not unusual to pay labor negotiators over a hundred dollars per hour for both their preparation and their time spent at meetings.

The active participation of board members at the table is a controversial issue. If a board member is part of the team, it is usually primarily as an observer. Only in some smaller districts is it likely that a board member will take an active role in negotiating a contract. Whoever is on the team must regularly keep the board fully abreast of the progress of the talks. Nothing can divide a district as quickly as conflict-riddled contract negotiations. For the same reason, board members might resist the temptation to become overly involved. Superintendents also might wish to stay somewhat above the struggle. A superintendent who can emerge as a peacemaker rather than the chief combatant will be in a better position to lead the district once a settlement has been reached.

Especially near the end of the process, contract negotiations can be an unpleasant and stressful time for all of the involved parties. Employee groups who are unhappy with the district's position have sometimes picketed the homes and businesses of school board members. Angry words could also appear in the local newspapers. It is often a time when the cohesiveness of the board and its administrators is severely tested. Board members must make a conscious effort not to let the process create personal antagonism toward union members. While trying to control the emotional effects of a difficult negotiation, everyone should remember the impact of the process on the children and the community. Many who have experienced difficult negotiations would agree that board members can maintain a better perspective if they are not personally participating in the actual talks.

During this process, there also is the issue of confidentiality. Board members must be extremely careful to keep secret the district's position on the issues. Individual members should not attempt through their own personal efforts to bring about a settlement through diplomacy without the permission of the entire board. When the district is engaged in negotiations, it is very helpful if board members can maintain a "solid front" for the district's positions in public. Decisions on possible compromises can be fought out in executive session. Union tactics will sometimes include efforts to split the board. As a result, individual members must constantly be aware that anything they say to a friend or family member could find its way to those on the other side of the table. In addition, board members must be extremely careful of anything that is said to a representative of the media. During negotiations, there should be one designated spokesperson for the school district. As a district passes through a period of protracted negotiations, it must be remembered that "this too will pass." With this in mind, board members must avoid saying or doing anything that will make the healing process more difficult.

There is no question that teacher unions and contract negotiations have placed additional stress on the relationship between boards of education and all of the employees of the district. As mentioned earlier, it is true that teacher unions are making a conscious effort to improve the process in many areas. Bob Chase, president of the NEA, has said to school boards and administrators that his organization "pledges to engage you in a new partnership—at the bargaining table and in our day-to-day relationship—aimed at transforming the quality of our schools."[19] There has probably never been a better time in recent years for school boards and teacher unions to reach out to each other.

In seeking an improved relationship and a true partnership, it will be best for the board to seek ways to involve teachers in the decision-making process. Faculty members need to be part of advisory committees planning new buildings or selecting new administrators. Boards should invite teachers to meetings to make presentations and continually seek ways to demonstrate the district's appreciation for outstanding contributions that teachers make to the district. The district should be a participant in teacher appreciation days. It also helps if board members mix with faculty at school events. Any district will benefit if the faculty sees the board of education as a group of people who appreciate the hard work that teachers do and who sincerely care about teacher input in decision making.

Along with the faculty, every school district has a large number of staff or support personnel. This group includes secretaries, teacher aides, bus drivers, maintenance personnel, and those who work in the school cafeteria. In some communities, these individuals are part of one bargaining group or they may be divided into a number of separate organizations. They may be part of a national union or a locally formed unit. Most often, the vast majority of these employees are district residents and taxpayers. Unfortunately, in too many school districts, these individuals are being paid less than they might be receiving in comparable jobs in the public sector. Because they are frequently loosely organized on a local basis, they are often not nearly as demanding as the teacher unions. As a result, boards have sometimes been somewhat heavy-handed in their treatment of these valuable and essential workers. In many districts, talented and conscientious teacher aides who are working directly with children are paid at or just above the minimum wage. Such treatment has caused a number of nonteaching employee groups to seek the help of various national unions. Equitable and fair treatment of these employees will not only ensure better morale in the district but also may help a system avoid the incursion of national unions, as well as high turnover.

As with the district's teachers, ways need to be found to recognize outstanding service by nonteaching employees. Some districts include a regular feature in the district newsletter that recognizes the contribution of an individual staff member each month. The board should consider sending letters to staff members who have performed a specific accomplishment. On occasion, it can be appropriate to honor individuals for outstanding service at a public board meeting. Recognition for passing milestones in years of service to the district is used by many school systems to show the district's appreciation. Sponsoring events such as an opening day luncheon for all employees can also be considered. Individual members of the board of education should personally pay attention to staff members' work when they visit a school building.

If the school looks bright and clean, complementing a custodian is an excellent way to show that district officials notice and care about good work.

Nonteaching personnel should be given opportunities for educational opportunities as part of their employment with the district. A workshop on assertive discipline can be very helpful for bus drivers. Secretaries need to be trained in new office technology. There are numerous ways that we can help our teacher aides to be more effective. Individuals who work directly with the children in a classroom should be compensated for taking college courses that help to make them more effective. All members of the staff should be considered for appointment to advisory committees. By recognizing and constantly demonstrating the board's support and appreciation of the work of nonteaching personnel, a district can help to ensure a better overall climate within the school system.

Whether it be a night custodian or the high school principal, a board of education can make a difference in how employees feel about their job. Even though unionism has created a more adversarial relationship in some districts, it is not impossible to maintain a high level of morale among district employees. It will not be easy, but it is most likely to occur in a district where the board of education views the district employees in a positive way. When this occurs, people will feel appreciated and will not hesitate to do their very best in performing their assigned functions. One of the most important functions of the faculty and staff is to help develop an effective budget. This important process will be the subject of the next chapter.

NOTES

1. Bob Chase, "The New NEA: Reinventing Teacher Unions for a New Era" 5 February 1997, www.nea.org/speak/npc_text.html (21 December 2000): 2.

2. Carol Chmelynski, "Districts Are Struggling to Hire Enough Teachers," *National School Boards Association School Board News*, 12 September 2000, www.nsba.org/sbn/00-sept/091200-1.htm (21 September 2000).

3. Adam Scott Gershenson, "Schumer: Bill to Add Teachers Likely to Pass," *The Journal News*, 9 December 2000, www.nyjournalnews.com/HomePage/120900/09shumer.html (16 December 2000).

4. Lynn Nordgren, *Education Update* 41, no.1 (January 1999): 7.

5. Jessica L. Sandham, "Calif. Groups Unite to Promote Peer Review," *Education Week* 19, no. 10 (3 November 1999): 18.

6. James B. Rowley, "The Good Mentor," *Educational Leadership* 56, no. 8 (May 1999): 21.

7. Rachelle Felier, Margaret Heritage, and Ronald Gallimore, "Teachers Leading Teachers," *Educational Leadership* 57, no. 7 (April 2000): 66.

8. "Board-Certified Teachers Outperform Others, Study Says," *American School Board Journal*, www.asbj.com/current/beforetheboard.html (16 December 2000): 1.

9. "Board-Certified Teachers," *American School Board Journal*.

10. David D. Haynes, "One Teacher's Experience with National Board Assessment, *Educational Leadership* 52, no. 6 (March 1995), www.ascd.org/readingroom.edlead/9503/haynes.html (21 December 2000): 1.

11. Lynn M. Cornett, "Lessons from 10 Years of Teacher Improvement Reforms," *Educational Leadership* 52, no. 5 (February 1995), www.ascd.org/readingroom/edlead/9502/cornett.html (21 December 2000): 4.

12. "Cincinnati School Board Approves Merit Pay Plan," *IASB School Board News Bulletin*, www.iasb.com/files/nb0600.htm (9 October 2000).

13. Richard Rothstein, "Merit Pay Won't Work," *American School Board Journal*, www.asbj.com/schoolspending/rothstein.html (16 December 2000): 1.

14. Rothstein, "Merit Pay," 6.

15. Sandra Feldman, "True Merit Pay," *American Teacher* 84, no. 7 (April 2000): 5.

16. Allan Odden, "New and Better Forms of Teacher Compensation are Possible," *Phi Delta Kappan* (January 2000): 362.

17. Odden, "New and Better," 363.

18. Dennis Sparks, "What Teachers Know and Don't Know Matters," *Harvard Education Letter* 15, no. 4 (July/August 1999): 8.

19. Chase, "The New NEA," 5–6.

CHAPTER 8

Budgets and Bond Issues

Even though school district employees do much of the day-to-day financial work, the board of education has the ultimate responsibility for creating the annual budget and for initiating and carrying out special bond issues. Because these are extremely important tasks, it is necessary for board members to have a general understanding of how school budgets are prepared. There is no single "right way" to develop a school budget. The procedure will vary from one community to another, but some steps are common to most school districts.

During the fall of each year, the administration should put together a budget calendar. This document should include all of the steps that must be taken in the preparation of the budget. It should list the responsible individual or group for each step, and a completion date for each item along with the calendar. It is advisable that during the first semester the entire school community should be actively involved in establishing long- and short-term district objectives. As mentioned earlier, this process should allow the participation of the administration, faculty, staff, and, of course, the board of education. The long-term objectives (three to five years) may remain the same as the previous year or they can be amended. At the same time, the board should be devising several specific goals for the coming year. For example, if the long-term objective of the district is to reduce average class size from twenty-seven to twenty, the goal for the coming year might be to ensure that classes in kindergarten through grade three are limited to twenty students. Objectives such as these need to be in place before budget decisions are made. Most of the money the district will spend each year is required to maintain the current program. Salaries and fringe benefits alone will take more than half of the budget. Supplies, equipment, utilities, and debt payments must also be part of any budget. Hopefully, after all of these constant items are budgeted, there will be some additional money available. This extra amount can be used to meet the objectives and goals that have been established. If there is little or no money left after meeting the needs for ongoing expenditures, the district can consider reductions in some of the flexible areas of the budget in order to finance the district's goals for the coming year. If raising reading scores is the objective, the board might have to consider cutting funds allotted for field trips or extracurricular activities in order to hire extra remedial reading teachers.

Early in the school year, the superintendent and the administrative staff can begin to make rough estimates of the probable revenues and needed expenditures for the coming year. Public schools in the United States receive almost all of their money from three sources. The two most important are aid from the state and money raised through local property taxes. With the exception of Hawaii, which is totally state funded, all school districts raise significant amounts of money locally. In most cases, this is done by individual districts, but in some states it is done on a county or regional basis. The federal government on average contributes only about 7 percent of the money for public schools. All of this aid is categorical in that it must be spent on specific programs. The largest single category is Title I aid, which is used to finance remedial programs. There are also financial aid and supplies for school breakfast and lunch programs. A significant portion of the federal aid to education is in the form of competitive grants. For instance, a school district could write a proposal that would fund the wiring of the school to allow students to utilize the Internet. Other kinds of grants, if approved, provide money for vocational education.

The administration of each school district must attempt to predict for the coming year both federal and state-aid funds that will be available for financing a proposed budget. This process is often very difficult because Congress and state legislatures may not yet have acted at the time when budgets are prepared. A well-informed superintendent will be constantly using numerous sources in order to make the most accurate possible prediction as to what federal state revenues are likely to be for the coming year. Before considering the local property tax levy that will be needed, the superintendent must first make a rough estimate of all other likely revenues. As part of the same process, an estimate should be made of proposed expenditures. Once this is done, it will be possible to determine what will be needed in property taxes. The result of these early calculations will often be alarming. Such a result is likely, especially if the administration is conservative in its prediction of federal and state aid. Such estimates should indeed be made carefully, as a school district can create serious problems if it guesses wrong on income for the coming year. Hopefully, there will be some surplus anticipated from the current year's budget that can be used as a cushion or for an additional revenue source. Board members need to be constantly aware of the fund balance that the district is maintaining. Administrators and boards of education can be criticized by both their auditors and the public for having either an overly large or little or no fund balance.

After these preliminary steps, the administration should ask principals to work with their faculty and staff to prepare building budgets. Directors of maintenance, transportation, and other special programs will also be given the opportunity to submit their own budget requests. In carrying out this process, the superintendent or chief business official will either allot a specific amount of money to each administrator or allow these individuals to submit all of the expenditures they feel are necessary. A compromise method is for the central administration to develop a form on which principals and other program directors include a ranking for their expenditure requests. While these individual school and department budgets are being prepared, the business department will also be calculating budget figures for salaries, debt payment, insurance, and other miscellaneous categories of expenditures that are necessary in any school district. A maintenance supervisor will be asked for proposed figures for utilities, maintenance and custodial supplies and equipment, contract services, and emergency funds for unforeseen maintenance problems. At the same time, the supervisor of transportation will be assigned budget lines for those expenditures necessary in this area.

It is advisable that a public budget hearing should be held during the early stages of budget preparation. This can be done either at a special meeting or as part of a regular board of education meeting. The purpose of such a hearing is to allow community members to have input into the budget before it is finalized by the board. These meetings also have the added benefit of providing the board the opportunity to gauge public sentiment concerning the upcoming budget. This is especially helpful in states where citizens actually vote to approve or disapprove a school budget.

On an established date, all of the budget requests will be submitted to the administration. Once all of the input has been gathered, a rough draft should be prepared and brought to the board of education. It is essential that, before being given a budget to evaluate, newly elected board members be given a thorough orientation on school budgets. Many of the terms used in preparing spending plans for schools may be unique. For instance, it is important to know the difference between "supplies" and "equipment." Board members should not be shy about asking questions. It is the board's duty to question both the revenue estimates and the proposed expenditures. At times, it may be necessary to ask for breakdowns of certain budget categories. If the maintenance department is requesting money for new equipment, board members should know what is included. It is possible that a majority of the board would prefer to spend money on library books rather than buffing machines. Although it sometimes happens, school administrators should not be overly sensitive to board members' questions or suggestions.

A public meeting or hearing might well be required prior to the adoption of the final budget. When holding a public budget meeting, administrators and board members should keep the following in mind:

1. The presentation should be clear and understandable to the public. (There should be handouts and visual aids.)
2. When possible, board members should play an active role in the meeting. The president of the board can preside and other board members could present sections of the budget and respond to questions and comments from the audience.
3. The board and superintendent should ensure that appropriate administrators and supervisors are available to answer specific questions.
4. If there is a question that neither an administrator nor a board member can effectively answer, citizens should be told that a re-

sponse will be forthcoming. "Shooting from the hip" can cause future difficulties for the leaders of the district. This is especially true if the board member or administrator is quoted in a local newspaper.

5. It is important to remain calm during public meetings. Antagonistic taxpayers will, on occasion, criticize district policies, as well as make personal attacks. When it is appropriate, school board members should support administrators or other school employees when they are unjustly criticized.

Once the board has approved a final budget document, it should be available to the public. Press releases for the local media must be clearly written. They need to emphasize the thoroughness of the budget preparation process, new initiatives that will be made possible by the budget, as well as cuts that have been made in various expenditure areas. Certainly, if the district has a newsletter, there should be a comprehensive article explaining the budget. Charts showing a breakdown of revenues and expenditures along with comparisons with the previous budget are helpful. It is not necessary to publish a complete line-by-line budget, but citizens should be given a telephone number to call if they have specific questions or desire to have a copy of the complete budget. An advantage of having the budget explanation as part of the newsletter is that the same issue can include some "good news" articles about what is happening in the district. For many readers of the school newsletter, the primary issue is how the budget will affect their property tax bills. Because it might well be impossible to predict the exact impact the budget will have on property taxes, the district must be especially cautious in how they deal with this question. When the district's projection concerning the impact of the budget on taxes is too low, it can create a credibility problem for the school district.

In communities where citizens vote on the budget, board members and administrators might also make an effort to make presentations on the budget to various community organizations. Explaining the budget to the community is a joint responsibility of board members and the administration.

The active participation of the board of education in the budget preparation process can occur at a number of stages. At the outset, the board is responsible for establishing the objectives and priorities for the budget. Some school boards play a very active role by establishing a budget committee to work with the administration. Although this can be very time consuming for a board member, it is the normal procedure in some districts. Such committees can meet with building administrators and department heads in order to better understand and analyze specific portions of the budget. At committee meetings, questions concerning line-item requests can be asked. In other districts, board members are responsible for making presentations on the budget at public hearings or to community groups. All board members will be expected to participate fully in discussions about the budget during several public board meetings. To properly carry out this function, school board members should insist that they be given the information necessary to make intelligent decisions in advance.

Along with preparing an annual budget, every school district will, on occasion, need to initiate a project that requires a public vote. Usually, this is made necessary by the fact that large amounts of money have to be raised to carry out the project. Many initiatives cannot be financed by the annual budget and this requires that the district receive the permission of the public to borrow large sums of money. In almost all cases, such borrowing requires a positive vote by the eligible voters in the district. For instance, a bond-issue vote might be required for a major maintenance project, such as new roofs or windows, additions to current buildings, or the construction of a new school. In all of these situations, the extra borrowing will most likely increase property taxes for a number of years.

Preparing a capital project bond issue requires a great deal of work by the school district. When a problem that may require a bond-issue referendum exists in a district, a board might wish to consider appointing an advisory committee to help with the process. Such a committee could include board members, representatives of the community, administrators, faculty, and staff. If the district wished to keep the faculty and staff in a separate committee, that could be an option as well. Any advisory groups established should be given a clear mission statement and specific guidelines. It must be made clear from the beginning that these committees are advisory and that all final decisions will be made by the board of education. When establishing such a group, the board should consider allotting a small amount of money for the committee. At the very least, the group should be provided refreshments at their meetings. It also might be helpful to allow committee members to visit other facilities at district expense.

If the project calls for new classrooms or a new building, it is essential that faculty members be actively involved. A district should not build a new shop, band room, or art room without gaining input from the teachers who will be using the room. Mistakes can be made if a board of education relies solely on the architect. Citizen groups also can include individuals who have specific expertise in certain aspects of a building project. Bankers, engineers, and contractors can all make valuable contributions during the planning process. In choosing community members to serve on an advisory committee, it is important that the board avoid selecting local individuals who might later be seeking contracts related to the project. It is essential that any possible claim of conflict of interest be avoided.

During the planning process, the board may decide to seek the assistance of a consultant or to enter into a contract with an architect. It must be made clear to the architect that the project cannot go forward until a positive vote of the public is gained. The financial planning of bond issues has become a very specialized field. Unless the school attorney has specific experience in this area, it is wise to consider employing a financial consultant. This person will not only help with planning and gaining public approval of the plan but will also assist in the sale of the bonds. An experienced consultant can help a district plan its future debt and help to ensure a successful bond sale.

As the plan for the bond issue is developed, a board of education might wish to hold a public hearing to inform the community of the initial plans. This should be done before the final plan is completed so that public input at the hearing can be considered. After such a hearing and when the advisory committee has completed its report, it will be up to the board to decide on the parameters for the project. The following questions will need to be answered. What is it that the district wishes to accomplish with the bond issue? How much is it likely to cost? What will be the duration of the bonds? What will be the impact of this project on the property tax rate while the bonds are being paid off?

Once the administration and the board have completed their work on the proposal, it must be explained to the voters. Just as with the budget, there must be press releases, newsletter stories, and district representatives who will give the speeches at public meetings. Often, board members can be effective advocates of proposed projects. This is especially true if the individual is a well-known and respected member of the community. The support of the project by a board member who is a prominent businessperson can have a much greater impact on voters than the words of a school administrator.

During the course of a campaign for a bond issue, many issues can arise. The district must be prepared with convincing arguments regarding the need, enrollment projections, and additional projects that might require borrowing in the near future. Questions that go unanswered from public meetings or letters to the local newspaper can turn voters against a proposal. If organized opposition arises in the community, ways must be found to respond quickly to those who are criticizing the project. Additional press releases or possibly a special newsletter might be necessary to thwart unfounded rumors or untrue statements made by the opponents of the project.

In gaining support for a bond issue, special attention should be given to several groups of voters. Although they represent perhaps only a third of those eligible to vote in most communities, parents of current and future students in the district have the most at stake. Presentations should be made at PTA meetings in the hope that interested parents will support the plan. Senior citizens will undoubtedly vote in large numbers and ways should be found to gain their support. If the proposal includes new athletic facilities or music rooms, sports and music booster clubs can become powerful advocates. Often they will initiate special mailings to their members or carry on telephone campaigns to get out the vote. Board members and administrators must be careful not to utilize school facilities or personnel in seeking support for a budget or bond issue. Giving out names, addresses, and telephone numbers of district residents should be avoided. Booster clubs and other supporters should not do their work on district phones and copy machines. The board of education's role is to present to the voters the information that they need to make an informed decision. That is not to say that the board cannot encourage citizens to come out to vote. One technique that is often used is to schedule school activities on the day of a vote. A spring concert or an athletic awards banquet will ensure that many parents are in the building on the night of the vote. If you decide to have an event at the same time as voting, be sure that you have adequate and convenient parking reserved for those who have come to vote. This is especially true in the case of senior citizens who might have difficulty walking longer distances. In any case, provisions should be made to make voting as easy and convenient as possible. It is also important that voting take place in a setting that is appropriate. Voters should not be forced to walk through the student corridors during the time when classes are passing or use a student lavatory that might smell of cigarette smoke.

Especially if the vote is scheduled in the spring or summer, districts should not ignore the eighteen-year-old voters who are still in school. Presentations on the bond-issue vote can be made during a senior social studies class to ensure that eligible student voters understand the proposal. It would be hoped that those students who are graduating from the school would be supportive of projects designed to improve their school.

Despite the best efforts of the board and the school administration, some bond-issue initiatives will fail. After a long campaign, such a result can be very disappointing. District officials cannot afford to merely sulk because of the defeat but rather must become proactive in attempting to discern the reason for the defeat. Because the problems that created the need for the bond issue are still present, the district must formulate a new strategy. This may require a survey or another public hearing to determine the best course of action.

If the bond issue was successful, the district can look forward to a busy and somewhat difficult period during which the project will be implemented. If the architectural firm has not been chosen, this will be the first task of the board. An advisory committee can be used to recommend a limited number of firms to be interviewed by the board. The superintendent and other administrators could also carry out this task. A key aspect of the selection process will be to carefully check the references of the firms being considered. It might be helpful for those screening the competing companies to view some of their completed projects. Other school administrators who have worked with the architects should certainly be consulted. Choosing an architect with significant experience working on schools is often helpful. Districts should seriously consider companies that have their own engineering departments. This can save some confusion in coordinating construction.

On many larger projects, the school should consider employing an independent clerk of the works to represent the school during the construction phases of the project. This knowledgeable individual should be an experienced construction specialist who will be present on site during the entire project to ensure that the plans are being followed. A clerk of the works is especially necessary if there is no one on the maintenance staff with significant experience in working with architects, engineers, and contractors.

During the construction stage, there will undoubtedly be a number of unforeseen problems. Decisions will have to be made that will result in "change orders." These alterations in the original plans usually mean an additional expense for the district. In the project budget, funds will be set aside for such changes but a district needs to be very careful that these change orders do not create cost overruns. Board members should be kept informed of major construction problems that arise. When there are decisions that will significantly affect the project, the board of education should participate. Since most likely as a board member you have helped to plan and promote the bond issue, the credibility of the board is at stake.

An outside accounting firm will audit bond issues, like every other phase of the business operation. The board of education has the responsibility to appoint the individual or firm who will do the annual audit. Effective auditors develop a trusting relationship with the board and help board members understand their reports. A good auditing firm will also make recommendations that can improve the business practices of the district. The annual audit report can be very complicated to those with little or no accounting background. Board of education members have an obligation to the community to understand and review carefully the annual audit and to ask the hard questions that need to be asked. A typical issue would be the question of why a district was not earning a reasonable rate of interest on money that was not immediately needed. Districts are paying substantial fees to auditing firms and, in too many cases, their reports are not being carefully considered by the elected representatives of the community.

Across the country there have been many examples of districts that have not used their funds wisely; in some few cases, there has been fraud and other "white-collar" crime. School boards have the important role as a "watch dog" of the funds managed by the districts. To do so effectively, a board member must first become informed about budgets, bond issues, and audit reports. As with other issues, it is the role of the board of education to question and make suggestions as to how the financial systems of the district can be improved. Ignoring this phase of the operation would indeed be a disservice to one's responsibility to the community. Meeting the responsibility of a board of education in financial matters is only one of the ways to ensure an effective and ethical board of education.

CHAPTER 9

Effective and Ethical School Boards

Successful boards of education are those whose members think of themselves as part of a team of individuals who are working to provide the best possible education for every student being served by the district. Although the school board has the primary responsibility for creating policy, a district will never reach its potential unless all of the stakeholders are cooperating to achieve excellence. Just as a superb faculty needs the support of the nonteaching staff, administration, and the board, a school board cannot be effective without conscientious and committed employees who care deeply about the children of the community. In creating a cooperative environment, the school board does a great deal in setting the tone for the district. If a board is seen as divided in their approach or less than concerned about or supportive of district employees, a trusting relationship will not develop.

Maintaining a positive image with employees and the community is a major challenge for a board of education. Any group of elected officials is bound to have differences of opinion about the best way to move a district forward. In some communities, these differences result in shouting matches at public meetings and with board members denouncing each other in the media. Even though occasional conflict is inevitable on any board, public meetings need to be orderly and civil. Although various state laws place restrictions on "executive sessions" or meetings which bar the public, every state allows such meetings for specific purposes. The law allows boards to meet privately to discuss sensitive personnel questions, contract negotiations, and other subjects where secrecy might be essential. When they do occur, these private meetings offer a time when board members can speak frankly about their concerns. The top administrators in the district should also be included in these sessions unless there is a good reason for excluding them. Nothing causes a superintendent more anxiety than not to be asked to participate in a meeting of board members. If anyone who is usually a part of public board meetings is kept out of an executive session, he or she should be given an explanation.

Private meetings of board members not only must be in keeping with state law and district policy but the privilege should not be abused. A board of education is an elected public legislature and citizens therefore have the right to observe board meetings when actions are taken. When a board member casts a vote, it must be in public because the voters have the right to know how each member votes on every issue. Boards who too often appear to be doing the district's business behind closed doors will be in danger of severe criticism. Every board member should be aware of the state laws governing executive sessions and public meetings. This includes the requirements for advance notice of all meetings and complete minutes which must be made available to citizens upon request. Many boards have had their actions reviewed by the courts when individual citizens have charged that the school district violated the laws regulating public meetings.

Some boards make the mistake of entering an executive session for hours during a regular meeting while the audience, who has come to the public meeting, is forced to wait without knowing when or if the board will return to public session. If it is necessary during a public meeting to enter executive session, the board should announce publicly the approximate length of the session and whether business will be conducted later in the meeting. It is better, if possible, to schedule executive sessions either prior to the public meeting or after the close of the regular meeting.

Observers of a public meeting can tell a great deal about how a board functions. Do the members treat each other, the public, and the administration in a friendly and polite manner? Are visitors to the meeting made to feel welcome with a handout that includes the agenda, identification of those participating in the meeting, and an explanation of any special rules used for conducting business? Is the room set up so people can see and hear without difficulty? Does it appear that certain board members or administrators dominate the discussion? Have board members done their homework and do they appear to understand the issues under discussion?

An effective board will be one that, during their public meetings, demonstrates that they and the school administration are working together not only to manage the school system but also to improve it. It will be clear that they are people who respect each other and who are listeners as well as talkers. A poorly organized and divisive public meeting sends the wrong message to the staff and community. There will be spirited debate, but there is no need for anger and disrespect. It is not necessary or probably even advisable for a board to be unanimous on every issue, but when there are differences, school board members must model ways to solve their internal disagreements without creating a spectacle.

One major danger for board members is the temptation during public meetings to "play to the audience." This tendency has become more common in communities where meetings are being broadcast on radio or television. It is not unusual for there to be a person or persons on a board who knowingly or unknowingly seek the public spotlight. Sometimes, such individuals have political ambitions or they might just be trying to impress their own supporters. When this occurs, it is up to the other members of the board to express their concern to the offending individual. Assuming that the problem is not with the board president, he or she is probably in the best position to speak to the member whose behavior is proving to be unsettling to the rest of the board.

The president is a key figure in helping to make the board an effective team. In choosing the individual who will conduct meetings, there are a number of qualities and skills that members should seek in their leader. Hopefully, a president will have had several years of experience as a board member prior to assuming this important leadership role. It is essential that this person be respected and trusted by not only fellow members but also by the employees and the community. As one of the chief spokespersons of the district, the president should be articulate and sincere when communicating with others. If there are extreme differences between board members, the president might best be a moderate. At the same time, the individual does not have to be the most creative thinker on the board, but should be logical and well organized.

Perhaps one of the most important attributes would be that the individual is a good listener who, after hearing differing opinions on an issue, can bring people together. Finally, the president must be a strong individual who will be able to stand up to disorderly citizens, an angry board member, or an overbearing superintendent. Few individuals have all of these characteristics, but they should be considered when deciding on the best candidate. There are boards that attempt to rotate leadership positions. Sometimes when a member is selected as vice-president, it is automatic that they will be the next president. A board should be very careful with such practices. The wrong person in the job can have an adverse effect on how the whole group is perceived by others and, in the end, cause the school board to be less effective.

Even with strong leadership, the work of a board can be undermined unless all of the members understand their roles. One requirement of an effective board member is the ability to keep confidential certain information. When the district develops its position for negotiating with an employee union, individual board members cannot talk about this issue with anyone other than their fellow members and school administrators. Unauthorized conversations can create major problems for the district's negotiating team. In some districts, individual board members have attempted to bring about settlements outside of formal negotiations and have merely complicated the process. As a member of a public body, board members are party to confidential information about employees. A board member who has a tendency to gossip can create havoc in a school district. New members must be carefully instructed about the fact that there will be certain information that cannot be shared.

A board can achieve absolute confidentiality, have well-organized meetings, excellent leadership, and still fail to be effective. Recently, more and more attention has been placed on the necessity of ethical behavior by elected officials. As a result, both the national and state school board associations have created codes of ethics. Some individual school districts have created their own codes. All of these documents have certain similarities.

The Texas Association of School Boards Code of Ethics is typical. The code calls for "equity in attitude," which is explained as the need to be fair and impartial in all decisions and actions. It implies that board members will not be prejudiced for or against any particular individual or groups. "Equity in attitude" also means that board members will give to others the respect that they wish to receive. Finally, this section of the code suggests that it is necessary to have an open mind on all issues brought before the group.

"Trustworthiness in stewardship" is defined as the need for board members to "ensure prudent and accountable use of district resources."[1] The concept of stewardship responsibility raises the issue of "conflict of interest," which is addressed in every code of ethics document. Many opportunities for potential conflicts of interest arise for board members, and this is especially true in a small community. A businessperson on the board may have sold products to the school district or a member could be in the position of having to vote on the employment appointment of a family member. The issue can also be as simple as board members having to vote on a program that would specifically benefit their own children. Such votes might appear to some citizens as a conflict of interest, even if they are not. A board member who is a teacher working in another district and is a member of the National Education Association will be in a position to vote on the local school district teacher contract, which is being signed with an affiliate of this union. Although this is not legally a conflict of interest, some community critics will conclude that the teachers on the board are taking care of their fellow union members.

With any potential conflict of interest, it is usually wise for a board member to not only abstain from voting but also not take part in the discussion prior to the vote. This is especially true if the district is considering the appointment of a relative of a board member. Because conflict of interest is a legal as well as an ethical issue, there will be times when an attorney should be consulted. Anytime the district is doing business with a firm owned or managed by a board member, a lawyer's opinion should be sought. The same is true with services that the school district is contracting. For example, a board member might be a member of an accounting firm that is auditing the district's finances. The decision on whether or not this is a conflict of interest may well depend on the specific position the board member has in the firm. All of these possible complications are serious matters that boards should consider carefully.

Codes of conduct frequently use such words as integrity and honor. In Texas, the code calls for board members to "tell the truth." Seemingly, this is a straightforward ethical issue, but it is not always as easy to carry out as it would seem. Anyone who has been involved in negotiations of any kind knows that the "game" often requires participants to hide their final position on issues. A district negotiating team that hopes to settle a contract by granting a 4 percent increase is not likely to offer that figure at the first negotiating session. The same might be true if the board is seeking to purchase a parcel of land for expansion. There are administrators and board members who are very uncomfortable in negotiations when the process requires them to make less-than-truthful statements. Others find playing the game much like bluffing in a poker game. Not every board member should become actively involved in negotiations.

There are other times when school districts are tempted to be less than totally truthful. The wording used on public statements regarding the impact of budgets and bond issues on the tax rate offers the opportunity to not tell the whole story. This is especially true when the board and administration are committed to gaining public approval of a proposal. Businesses and politicians face the same dilemmas with their advertising campaigns. School districts that stretch the truth or omit relevant information are not acting in an ethical manner. Individual board members sometimes need to remind each other that they should tell the "whole truth," even if it hurts the objective that they are seeking.

Our nation's democratic system is based on the rule of law. School districts must obey federal, state, and local statutes and policies. There will be many times when board members will disagree vehemently with laws and regulations. Such a situation could occur regarding certain mandates for dealing with private and religious schools. Some board members may have a problem with the idea that the district must pay for transportation and textbooks for these schools. On the other hand, another board member might object to court decisions that forbid a principal to lead a public prayer over the public address system. Board members may be angry enough about laws or court decisions and wish to disobey or ignore the troublesome mandate. Civil disobedience is one way to change unpopular laws, but a school district should be very cautious about ignoring the law. Such actions can lead to severe penalties. It is also true that an elected body, which also develops its own policies and rules, can establish a negative model in a district if it ignores mandates from other governments. This does not mean that a school board should not be active in lobbying legislators on issues facing school districts. Like telling the truth, it is important that boards consistently uphold the laws governing public education.

Integrity as an elected official also requires that board members remain independent and not "surrender judgment" to any individual or group at the expense of the district as a whole.[2] During election campaigns, board members may receive financial support and assistance from taxpayer groups or friends. At every level of representative government, there will be people who attempt to influence an elected official's vote. Some of your supporters will feel that they have earned the right to have you at least listen to them. Board members should be good listeners whether the person is a supporter or someone who opposed your election. An ethical board member cannot become a tool of any specific individuals or groups. It is essential that elected representatives of the community be independent enough to judge every issue on its merits.

There has long been a divergence of opinion over whether legislators are obligated to vote on any issue based primarily on the opinions of the majority of their constituents or whether an elected representative should vote based on his or her own conscience and personal views. Because board members have much more information on some issues than the general public, there will be times when representatives will be tempted to vote their own views even though they might be unpopular in the district. In his book *Profiles in Courage*, John Kennedy defines courage in the words of Ernest Hemingway as "grace under pressure." There will be times when school board members have the opportunity to display this type of courage.

During a board member's tenure in office, it is also important that he or she be committed to his or her own personal continuing education. This means reading, attending school events, and participating in workshops designed specifically for board members. Having taken on the responsibility of serving on a school board, a person should give all meetings a high priority. Many board members have busy schedules, but outside of their own family obligations and perhaps an occasional conflict due to their work schedule, board meetings should have top priority. It is a time-consuming commitment, but one should not take it on unless he or she is willing to spend the time necessary.

In thinking about the role of a board member, one should consider it primarily as a way to serve one's community. To use board membership merely to flatter one's ego or to accomplish a single objective is unfair to your colleagues on the board, the school employees, and most of all, to the children of the district.

Finally, although board members are responsible to the whole community, they should be continually guided by asking what is best for the students of the school district. Anyone who is not committed to improving the educational possibilities for children should choose another way to serve their community.

At the beginning of this chapter, it was noted that to have an effective and ethical board of education, there must be a team approach. In New York State, this fact was underlined when the New York School Board Association and the New York State Council of School Superintendents adopted jointly the code of ethics shown in table 9.1.

Table 9.1   Joint Code of Conduct

1. Assure the opportunity for high-quality education for every student and make the well-being of students the fundamental principle in all decisions and actions.
2. Honor all national, state, and local laws and regulations pertaining to the education and public agencies.
3. Represent the entire community without fear or favor, while not using these positions for personal gain and accepting all responsibilities as a means of unselfish service.
4. Uphold the principles of due process and individual dignity, and protect the civil and human rights of all.
5. Adhere to the principle that the board shall confine its role to policy making, planning, and appraisal while the superintendent shall implement the board's policies.
6. Act as part of an educational team with mutual respect, civility, and regard for each other's respective responsibilities and duties, recognizing that the strength of a school board is in acting as a board, not as individuals; and that the strength of the superintendent is in being the educational leader of the school district.
7. Practice and promote ethical behavior in the boardroom and in the classroom. Maintain high standards and the effectiveness of education through research and continuing professional development.
8. Consider and decide all issues fairly and without bias.
9. Instill respect for community, state, and nation.
10. Protect the spirit and letter of all contracts until fulfillment or modification by mutual agreement.
11. Inspire and nurture the highest level of ethics and integrity.[1]

1. "Joint Code of Conduct," *New York State School Boards Association*, <"http://www.nyssba.org/ bdsupport/jcoc.html" www.nyssba.org/bdsupport/jcoc.html> (8 September 2000).

It is certainly true that a school cannot truly achieve excellence unless it is managed and administered by ethical board members and administrators. Such a team that is also well organized and has skilled leadership can and will be a positive force in any community. Such boards are impossible to develop unless the school district is able to enlist the services of talented and honest candidates who truly wish to serve the children of the district. Even when such people step forward, it is essential that the district provide ongoing training for its elected representatives. If this is done, the board, along with the school administration, can forge and implement a vision for their community which will ensure the best possible education for the children of the district.

NOTES

1. "Code of Ethics for Board Members," *Texas Association of School Boards*, http://www.tasb.org/boards/boards_ethics.html (9 October 2000).

2. *Texas Association of School Boards*.

CHAPTER 10

Working with the Community

"It takes the whole village to educate a child" is the African proverb that Hillary Rodham Clinton chose to use as the title of her book on public education. Increasingly, professional educators, local government agencies, and the business community are accepting the fact that schools alone cannot solve the multitude of problems facing our nation's children. As a result, school boards and administrators are reaching out to their communities to not only receive input from district citizens but to actively cooperate with businesses and government agencies to improve schools.

In every school district, there are many individuals and groups who have a sincere interest in the education of the children of the community. Many of these groups have very specialized concerns. Most districts have a Parent Teacher Association, as well as sports and music booster clubs. There are often organizations of parents of children with learning disabilities or attention deficit disorders. In some places, there are parents who support additional programs for gifted and talented children. Senior citizens' organizations and taxpayer leagues can become "watch dogs" of the financial decisions made by the board of education. Any problem that arises in the district can lead to the formation of an ad hoc group of citizens. An act of violence in a school will often cause the formation of a group of concerned citizens. The business community also periodically demonstrates an active interest in schools. A larger than usual tax increase could activate the local Chamber of Commerce. Sometimes churches will become involved in controversial issues that arise. Members of any of these groups may, from time to time, attempt to directly influence the decisions of board members. Because of the tremendous public interest in schools, boards and administrators are beginning to think more like private businesses.

We now hear educators talking about marketing and customer service at board meetings. Attention is being paid to making schools less bureaucratic and more welcoming. Lyn Chambers reminds school district employees "that you never get a second chance to make a first impression."[1] It is important to ask whether your school has a warm, cordial, and concerned person answering the phone, or are parents and other citizens attempting to deal with an impersonal answering service. It is essential that any visitors to the school be treated in a polite, helpful, and considerate way. When one enters a school, is the building clean, well cared for, and colorful? Is there student work displayed? Do the board and administration pay adequate attention to the exterior of their buildings and are school grounds well maintained? School district residents should be proud of their schools and enjoy visiting them.

It is also important that school districts communicate effectively on a regular basis with district citizens. A school newsletter that is published regularly and sent to all of the homes in the community is probably the best way to keep the public informed. Most districts have some kind of newsletter, but the frequency and quality vary greatly. Many boards have found that readers take their newsletter more seriously if it is attractive and colorful, and if it includes pictures, charts, and possibly even cartoons. A professionally printed newsletter is much more costly, but is usually more widely read. There are a number of features that should be considered for inclusion in an effective school newsletter. Some of the more common types of information are listed below.

1. a complete calendar of school-related events, with the location and time for each (In some districts where there are no other means of communicating information on events, the board of education can offer to print in its newsletter other meetings and events taking place in the community.)

2. articles featuring upcoming programs (For example, if the high school is presenting a musical or concert in the near future, a story could be written to publicize the event.)

3. special honors achieved by students (Among the honors to be considered would be the publication of the honor rolls in all of the district schools.)
4. board of education minutes or an article summarizing board of education news (A board president might also wish to have a regular column to keep the community informed concerning activities of the board.)
5. stories giving information about new employees
6. recognition of employees or outstanding students (Perhaps there could be a regular feature that recognizes the staff member, faculty member, or student of the month.)
7. information about the annual budget or bond issues
8. stories about student academic achievement, including student test results
9. articles about the sports teams, musical groups, or other extracurricular activities

In producing a district newsletter, it should be remembered that the purpose is to provide information. The prose should not read as mere propaganda or in a way that the school district is attempting to put a "positive spin" on every subject. It is essential to the credibility of the publication that the articles not be seen as a "slick" effort to convince the public that they have a perfect school system. If there are problems in the district, they can and should be addressed in a district publication. The newsletter can be used to ask the help of the community in solving a problem. A school district newsletter can be "upbeat" and interesting without being overly "syrupy."

A newsletter is only one of many ways that a school district can communicate with the residents of the community. Newspapers and radio and television stations often are interested in the activities and business workings of the district. Representatives of the media are sometimes thought of by administrators and board members as being "the enemy." The fact is that these individuals have a professional obligation to report the truth about what is occurring in schools. It is far better to attempt to develop a trusting relationship with the reporters who are responsible for covering a school district rather than trying to control what they include in their stories. If reporters attend board meetings, they should be provided a comfortable place to take notes or to record the meeting. When background material is not confidential, reporters can be given copies to help them complete their stories. It should be expected that reporters will be looking for conflict at board meetings and that serious differences of opinion that are expressed publicly are likely to be in the headlines. With this in mind, board members must constantly remember that they will receive much better coverage if they treat each other with respect and avoid personal attacks.

In many districts, either the president of the board or the superintendent is designated as the chief spokesperson with the media. Having too many people giving interviews or talking to the press can send a divided message to the community. This is especially true if the district is facing a difficult issue such as a stalemate in negotiations with the teachers' union. At a time like this, one person should be given the responsibility for articulating the board's position.

When a reporter or an editor writes something that is critical of the board of education or the district as a whole, a response is sometimes necessary. Although it is tempting to react by reducing the newspaper's access, this would likely cause the relationship to deteriorate further. If the editorial or story contains untruths, the board might wish to prepare a "letter to the editor." This is potentially a dangerous practice, as it can lead to an unending series of articles and responses. Other ways to respond to unfair coverage in the media would be to prepare a press release or to write an article for the school newsletter. Most newspapers and radio and television stations will consider a press release that they deem represents news that their customers will find interesting.

In addition, school districts should, on a regular basis, be notifying the media of school activities that are open to the public and about providing any positive press releases relating to students or faculty. There should be specific administrators and staff who have as part of their responsibility creating news releases that will show the school in a favorable light. Reporters should be regularly invited into the schools to view projects that might be of interest. If there is a group of high school students who are participating in a mock trial or a model United Nations program, the media should be asked to attend. Reporters and editors should be invited to participate in career days and to speak in appropriate classes. Whenever possible, a student-prepared page can be printed in the local newspaper. Photographs should be taken at school events and made available along with the appropriate story for the local newspapers. In dealing with representatives of the media, the school district should seek to create a relationship that is characterized by trust and cooperation. This will not occur if a district tries to maintain absolute control over what is reported or if school officials are less than open with those assigned to cover the school news.

The time when boards of education are most on display for the public is at their regular meetings. The times and locations of public meetings of any municipal legislature must be well advertised and district citizens should be encouraged to attend. Districts should go out of their way to make their visitors comfortable. This means that the audience should be able to see and hear the proceedings. Anyone attending a meeting should be provided an agenda. It is also an excellent practice to give members of the audience a handout identifying members of the board and administration. This pamphlet could include pictures of each of the participants in the meeting and explain the rules governing the meeting, as well as a list of the primary functions of a board of education.

Many boards set aside time for visitors to speak. Sometimes a district will limit the length of statements that can be made during this portion of the meeting. Other districts require that those who wish to address the board sign up prior to the meeting. There will be times when board meetings are very well attended. This most often occurs when the board is discussing a controversial issue. When administrators expect a large crowd, special attention should be given to insure that the meeting will be orderly. Ensuring that public meetings are well planned is only one way that a board of education can maintain a positive image in the community.

It is frequently helpful for a school district to target certain interest groups in order to maintain community support. Senior citizens have several special reasons for being interested in schools. Along with the fact that they may have grandchildren in attendance, they also may be more interested than others in the property tax rate. Because many older individuals have fixed incomes, an increase in their property tax could have a major impact on them. It is also true that some older people believe that many of the extracurricular programs offered by the schools are unnecessary and might be considered as "frills."

There are a number of ways this group of voters can be made to feel better about the taxes they are paying. Continuing education programs using school facilities are popular in many districts. Offering free or inexpensive night or weekend courses in computer technology or physical fitness can allow older people to benefit from the school facilities. A number of schools have opened their doors in the early morning to allow senior citizens to get their daily exercise by walking the halls before the students arrive. Special grandparents' days have been initiated in some schools. Making available to senior citizens free passes to school events also often provides an enjoyable night out during which our older citizens see young people engaged in wholesome and constructive activity. If there are senior citizen organizations that meet in the school district, administrators and board member should be available as speakers. For senior citizens, as for other members of the community, volunteer programs can be established. Many older people enjoy helping out in the school office, library, and the classroom.

Volunteers can be sought not only from the ranks of our older citizens but also from parents. Of all the groups in any community, the parents of the students have the most intense and immediate interest in the schools. Districts must do everything possible to gain the support of the parents of the community. To be a positive force in a school, the activities of volunteers must be carefully monitored. Specific policies must be developed. In creating a program, the following factors should be kept in mind:

1. A volunteer program should have a specific person assigned to administer the recruitment, training, and the assessment of all volunteers.
2. All potential volunteers must be interviewed and screened to determine their strengths and weaknesses. Acceptable placement of volunteers depends upon a careful assessment of each individual.
3. There must be a planned program of orientation and training for all volunteers.
4. There should be a performance assessment process in place. On rare occasions, it will be necessary to discontinue the service of

a volunteer for being undependable or displaying inappropriate behavior.

5. There should be a plan for regularly recognizing the work of volunteers. A volunteer appreciation dinner would be an appropriate time for awarding certificates to recognize the many hours that volunteers have spent working in the school.

6. Especially for senior citizens, a volunteer program might consider providing transportation for volunteers.[2]

In a large study on volunteer programs, Brian O. Brent concluded that "every school can benefit from a thoughtfully planned, organized, and focused volunteer program."[3]

Volunteer programs are only one way to build parental support for schools. Teachers must report regularly to parents. Frequent progress reports and understandable report cards should be sent on a regular basis. These forms can be made "user friendly" and should not be characterized by vague educational jargon. It is also important that the school frequently report positive news as well as problems. Teachers and principals should be encouraged to make "happy calls" or to write notes to praise a student for outstanding work.

The board of education and the professional staff should be actively involved with parents' organizations such as the PTA. School personnel can provide many of the programs for these meetings. The board might also cooperate with the PTA in cosponsoring a "candidate's night" at which those seeking election to the board can express their views. Administrators and board members should be available to give reports and provide programs on the school budget or upcoming bond issues. It is also important that districts utilize the special talents of citizens in the community for advisory committees. In recent years, businesses have been increasingly interested in schools.

Local alliances between community businesses and schools have been formed in many districts. These groups have been active in planning career days, during which representatives of many occupations come to school to speak to interested students. Time has been set aside during the school day for students to go out into the community to participate in work-study or in "shadowing" programs. Businesses have allowed their employees to become mentors and tutors for students of all ages. An example of such a program would be the relationship established between the New York City School District, the Junior Achievement Organization, and the investment firm Goldman Sachs. Two thousand of the companies' employees have been allowed to go into the public schools to teach about business.

> Lisandro Garcia-Marchi, the principal at P.S. 98, says the program "shows the kids that they are important. It gives them a taste of what the business world is about and a sense that they can join it." "In a lot of these neighborhoods, the most successful business person is the local drug dealer," says Peter Mertens, executive vice president of Junior Achievement. "Even a one-day visit shows the kids that not all successful white guys grew up rich, that women can get high-level jobs, that poor kids can have opportunities, too."[4]

On the other hand, some of the arrangements between businesses and schools have become very controversial.

> When the Colorado Springs, Colorado, school board negotiated a sponsorship contract in August 1997 with Coca-Cola worth up to $11.1 million over ten years, many critics raised objections about the increasing commercialization of public education. The contract gives the soft drink company exclusive access to vending machines in the schools and advertising signs on school busses and in hallways.

> Similar concerns were raised when US West committed $2 million and Pepsi Cola committed to $2.1 million to help the Jefferson County, Colorado, school district build two new football stadiums. The district gave Pepsi exclusive rights to sell its products in the district's schools. In return, Pepsi will give the district a fifty percent commission on its drink sales, estimated to be worth $700,000 a year, and will establish a scholarship fund, estimated at $48,000 a year.

> Members of both of these school boards also had reservations about the implications of these deals, and the boards carefully weighed the benefits and risks. In the end, both boards decided that the huge amount of money the schools will reap ultimately will benefit the academic program for the school children.[5]

Because of the obvious differences of opinion concerning such arrangements, school boards must be very selective and cautious in developing special arrangements with any business. There have also been numerous examples of companies voluntarily providing schools with equipment, such as computers and machinery for technology programs. There will continue to be many opportunities for districts to take advantage of the interest of the business community in providing better-prepared graduates.

School districts should also seek a positive relationship with the leaders of the other municipalities and the various programs that are being provided by local governments. Police officers and firefighters can not only offer protection to the schools but they can also provide effective instruction in areas such as drug abuse and fire safety. Nationwide, the police-sponsored DARE program has been introduced in thousands of districts. Schools are dependent on local government for water, sewer, and traffic safety in the areas around the buildings. Especially in northern climates, school officials must work closely with the local governments that are providing snow removal services. District employees must also develop a working relationship with agencies dealing with child abuse and probation. Because many of the social services departments are working directly with students and parents, there should be an established mechanism for continuous dialogue with appropriate school personnel.

In addition to the groups already mentioned, there are civic clubs that frequently seek to help the schools. It could be the American Legion wishes to hold their annual oratorical contest or a Rotary Club wanting to offer scholarships to needy students. Most often, these projects can provide valuable opportunities for children. Because the groups have very frequent meetings, they also provide the opportunity for the school to send out speakers or musical groups to provide programs. School board members who belong to such organizations should encourage school-related programs. Civic organizations often build school playgrounds, buy instructional equipment, and stock the shelves of school libraries. Board members should help to encourage these mutually beneficial projects.

School districts must also be sensitive to their relationship with the churches in the community. Although the rules governing the separation of church and state will affect some aspects of the relationship, public schools and churches can cooperate. To begin with, if there are private schools sponsored by churches in the district, public funds must be allotted to provide transportation, textbooks, and health and special education services. In carrying out this legal mandate, school districts can either forge an effective working relationship or create a situation characterized by frequent conflict. In the end, it is undoubtedly beneficial for the community if school districts attempt to establish a cooperative relationship with all of the private schools in their district. The same is true with the growing number of families who are homeschooling their children. Although the district has some legal responsibilities in regulating this practice, there is nothing to be gained by alienating these families by overregulation. With both church groups and home-schooling organizations, there is no legal reason to prevent board members or administrators from becoming speakers at their meetings. It is also useful to a school to consider appointing clergy to appropriate advisory committees. After a fatal accident or a suicide, some districts have invited clergy into the school to be available to talk with troubled students.

Whether it be church groups or other organizations in the community, it is wise for district officials to work diligently to ensure that schools are active and productive agencies in the community. With the help of a number of outside agencies, a school can actually become a true community center.

Rogers Elementary School, near downtown Stamford, Connecticut, receives its first pupils by 7:30 in the morning and sends home the last children at about 5:30 in the afternoon. Adults from the community are in the building for one program or another throughout the day, and children and their parents often return in the evening for various activities. Rogers pursues its widened mission through the Rogers School Community Center Organization (ROSCCO), which writes grants, receives funds, and operates a panoply of supplementary programs for the school and its neighborhood.

Rogers is unusual but not unique. Increasingly, schools around the country—especially those serving large numbers of students from economically disadvantaged backgrounds, as Rogers does—are widening their mission to encompass more aspects of a youngster's life. Often, this means reaching out to the entire family.[6]

In Rochester, New York, School #17 principal, Ralph Spezio, was successful in raising sufficient funds to build an all-purpose medical facility for his impoverished urban neighborhood. The building is located on the same campus as the elementary school. As an elected representative of the school district, school board members should become active participants in this type of cooperative relationship; at the same time, they should be encouraging district administrators to reach out to the larger communities. There is very little doubt in anyone's mind that at this point in our nation's history it does indeed take "the entire village to educate a child."

NOTES

1. Lyn Chambers, "How Customer Friendly Is Your School?" *Educational Leadership* 56, no. 2 (October 1998): 35.
2. Brian O. Brent, "What You Never Knew about School Volunteers," *The Education Digest* 66, no. 2 (October 2000): 55.
3. Brent, "What You Never Knew," 59.
4. Anne L. Bryant, "To Be Effective, School-Business Partnerships Should Boost Student Learning and Educate the Community," *School Board News*, 28 October 1997, http://www.asbj.com/achievement/sbsa/sbsa5.html (22 September 2000).
5. Bryant, "To Be Effective."
6. Gene Maeroff, "How Schools Nationwide Are Becoming Community Agencies—And Making Life Better for Needy Children," *The American School Board Journal*, 1998, http://www.asbj.com/achievement/sbsa4.html (22 September 2000).

CHAPTER 11

What Makes a Good School?

Working with the community and the professional staff are both ways that a board of education can achieve schools that are more effective. There are also many other initiatives that have been proven helpful to public schools. Even though innovation has been a constant trend in education, there has also been a continuous stream of criticism of our schools. A number of research projects have pointed the way for positive change in recent years.

In 1971, George Weber initiated a study that sought to determine what made certain schools more effective in encouraging successful student achievement at a high level. Perhaps the most influential single study in this effort was done by Ronald Edmonds. The research resulted in a "five-factor theory of effective schools."[1] Edmonds' work led to numerous articles and workshops in the 1980s as school districts attempted to use the research to improve their schools. The five factors identified in the study included the idea that an essential characteristic of effective schools is strong leadership. This and other studies have highlighted the need to have outstanding principals in our schools. Helping to select these individuals is an important task of the board of education. Studies show that students learn best when they attend schools in which the principal demonstrates the following characteristics:

- articulates a clear school mission
- is a visible presence in classrooms and hallways
- holds high expectations for teachers and students
- spends a major portion of the day working with teachers to improve instruction

- is actively involved in diagnosing instructional problems
- creates a positive school climate[2]

The second factor identified by Edmonds was that an effective school must have a clear mission. Developing such a statement for schools is much more difficult than one might expect. During the twentieth century, our public schools have been required to significantly expand their services to children. In part, this is because of the abdication of the family. Schools have taken on the role of teaching about sex, the dangers of drugs, good health practices, home economics, and in many cases, how to drive a car. In addition, we have moved into the area of vocational training for some and college-level courses for others. The impact of laws mandating special education services has created dramatic new demands on school programs. Along with teachers, our professional staff now includes numerous counselors, speech therapists, physical therapists, and social workers. At the same time, many communities have sought special options for gifted and talented students. Our secondary schools are expected to provide a large variety of extracurricular activities to help students develop social and leadership skills. Again, because of societal problems, we now have options for teenage mothers, school-sponsored latchkey programs, and we not only provide school lunches but a breakfast program as well. During the last decade, schools have been expected to take on much of the responsibility for computer training. Others have strongly urged that the curriculum seek to improve the values of our children through character education initiatives. We have also become extremely concerned about building a higher self-esteem in all of our students. It is no longer true that schools must just teach reading, writing, and arithmetic.

All of these possible functions make it extremely difficult for a school to articulate a clear and focused mission statement. Because of the many possible goals that can be considered, it would seem that to be meaningful, a school would have to make some choices when writing a mission statement. During the past decade, business organizations have been facing the challenge of developing mission statements. In many cases, it has been easier for some businesses to do so. For instance, Polaroid could agree on the following statement of organizational purposes. "Polaroid manufactures and sells photographic products based on inventions of the company in the field of one-step instant photography and light-polarizing products, utilizing the company's inventions in the field of polarized light. The company considers itself to be engaged in one line of business."[3]

A company like Central Soya can state its purpose in one sentence. "The basic mission of Central Soya is to be a leading factor in producing and merchandising products for the worldwide agribusiness and food industry."[4]

Writing mission statements became an essential part of the total quality management movement, which swept the country in the 1980s and 1990s. Business consultants worked with administrators and boards of education to help bring the principles of this popular philosophy to school districts. Still, because of the many expectations of schools, it was extremely difficult for educational institutions to state their missions in a few words. Committees of teachers and community members grappled with the task. Evenings were spent writing and rewriting two or three sentence paragraphs. Boards of education were always asked to approve of the final draft of these statements. Once completed, the district mission statement was printed and displayed in every school, and often in every classroom. Many schools publicize the statement by including it in every newsletter. Faculty and staff members were expected to use the statement as a guiding principle in carrying out their responsibilities in the district. A typical result was this statement, adopted by the Byron-Bergen Central School Board of Education in New York State.

> Together with the community and family, the Byron-Bergen Central School District will encourage its students to attain their optimum potential and become productive, responsible members of society. Self-esteem and mutual respect will be fostered in an environment of high moral and ethical values.

This very generalized statement was the result of hours of negotiations, which included discussions at board, PTA, and faculty meetings. During the process, individuals and groups were able to insert their favorite causes into the final draft. Unfortunately, because the statement contains a number of objectives, it is not as helpful as it might be in establishing a clear district mission. If the document said, "Our school will teach reading, writing, and arithmetic," it would be obvious to all concerned what the school was attempting to accomplish. It is doubtful that any public school will ever again be able to have such a limited and narrow purpose. Most likely, schools in the twenty-first century will undoubtedly be asked to do even more. Although the effective school movement emphasized creating a mission statement, it is perhaps questionable if this exercise has greatly affected what is actually occurring in our schools.

A third characteristic identified by the effective school research was that successful schools provide a "safe and orderly climate." The following statistics will highlight the need for the concern about this issue.

- For more than two decades, opinion polls have shown that the public considers lack of discipline to be among the most serious problems facing schools.[5]
- The National Institute of Education's Safe School study found that, in the late 1990s, only one in every fifty-eight schools reported crime to the police.[6]
- The National Parent-Teacher Association reported that the annual cost of vandalism, probably in excess of $600 million, is greater than the nation's total budget for textbooks.
- More than three million crimes occur on school grounds each year. That's sixteen thousand crimes a day.
- Each year, scores of students and teachers are killed by gunfire, hundreds are wounded, and hundreds more are held hostage.
- Almost one in six students reports being victimized on school property during any six-month period.
- Approximately one in ten high school students reports that he or she carried a weapon at least once during the past month.[7]

Schools that take the issue seriously have developed a number of ways to deal with the problem. Special staff, such as school psychologists and family social workers, and schoolwide initiatives to increase communication and reduce tension all are being used to prevent new school violence. Until recently, most Americans thought of school violence as being primarily a problem of our urban schools. During recent years, the headline incidents have nearly all occurred in rural and suburban areas. As a result, this characteristic of the effective school movement has become a major concern of all boards of education.

The fourth of the five factors of successful schools is that they make a conscientious effort to regularly monitor student progress. Such schools have clearly defined academic goals and mechanisms are in place to continually measure student learning. National norm-referenced tests, such as the Metropolitan Achievement Tests (MAT) and the Scholastic Assessment Tests (SAT) are used in many districts. Specific objective-referenced tests, such as the New York State Regents examinations, are used to gauge student mastery of specific bodies of knowledge. These tests, along with teacher-made tests, allow a district to track individual student progress and to develop appropriate remedial programs for those students who are not meeting academic expectations. In some schools, in addition to traditional testing, other alternative assessment measures have been developed.

One of the most popular techniques is the use of student portfolios. The state of Vermont has pioneered the use of portfolios as a way to evaluate student development of both skills and knowledge. These ongoing records of student work can also be used to diagnose a student's academic weaknesses. Whether it is by using portfolios or testing, it does seem that an ongoing assessment program would be necessary to ensure that students are reaching the academic goals of the district. Such a process would also allow schools to monitor and adjust their teaching methods and curriculums.

The final characteristic highlighted in the research is the need for schools to have high expectations of their students. For much of the twentieth century, many schools provided different curriculums for those students who might not be aspiring to a college education. These curriculums sometimes were "watered down" to the point where they failed to adequately challenge many students. Teachers would frequently have lower academic expectations for students who might attend vocational schools. In a 1969 study, the notion of a "self-fulfilling prophecy" was introduced. The conclusion of the researchers was that teacher expectations for students were highly correlated to what children actually learned.[8] Research such as this has helped to stimulate the movement towards higher academic standards for all children.

Although the effective school studies were important in shaping the educational reform movement in the 1980s and 1990s, the findings have not gone unchallenged. There has been criticism of the way that model schools were selected. It is difficult to develop a consensus among educators as to what is indeed an effective school. If one disagrees with the established ideal, the characteristics that are discovered are of little value. The designation of excellence can vary depending on whether the study is measuring purely academic achievement or whether factors such as student self-esteem, creativity, and leadership skills are considered. Another concern of the critics was that the research was conducted in elementary schools and therefore the results might not be as applicable in secondary schools.

As noted earlier, a number of other research-based factors can guide the thinking of board members as they seek to make their school system more effective. A subjective way of evaluating whether an individual school building is working well is to spend time visiting the school and talking with students, faculty, secretaries, and custodians. One gets a feel for a school by just listening in the faculty room or in the break room of the staff. Faculty rooms can be dismal places. Many student teachers are discouraged by the conversations they hear among teachers. Too often, the talk is dominated by bitter criticism of the school administration, board of education, or just petty gossip dealing with students, parents, and other district employees. Some of this type of discussion is inevitable, but in an effective school, there will be talk about teaching and ways to help individual children.

A school should be a happy place where all of the employees are able to work together and enjoy each other's company. One way to gauge whether a school has a positive environment is to watch the way that adults interact with children. Does the school feel more like a prison? In an article entitled "The Heart of School Leadership," a retired principal advises school leaders to "start by making your school community a family. Emphasize that all school populations—gifted and talented, parents and community, learning disabled, emotionally disabled—belong to one family that is working together, learning together, and sharing."[9]

In some schools, one can feel a high level of stress among students as well as staff. Within schools with such an environment, there will be an obvious lack of closeness among students and staff. The leadership of the district and the building are either feared or thought to be incompetent. Too many employees are not really enjoying their work in far too many schools. This unhappiness cannot help but have a negative effect on children. If a board member senses that there are problems within individual buildings within the district, it is essential that the issue be raised with the superintendent. At certain times, there are negative feelings present in each of the schools of the district. In such communities, the relationship between employees and the administration is characterized by frequent grievances and by long and bitter contract negotiations.

If such a climate persists over an extended period, the board of education must take action to improve relationships within the district. Often, the board itself is the focus of the negative feelings of employees. Instances of conflict are inevitable, especially during prolonged and bitter labor negotiations. If the relationship remains negative even after the resolution of the contract, a board must take action to bring the various components of the school district together. This is often very difficult if the board has developed negative feelings about the district's employees. To deal with such situations, the administration and the board of education should initiate an ongoing dialogue with the leadership of the employee groups. An attempt should be made to jointly develop a strategy for improving relationships. This will require board members who are willing to listen without being defensive. It will also mandate that these discussions be ongoing, rather than merely a one-time response to a problem.

Another practice that appears to have a very positive influence on schools is a continuous program of in-service training for faculty and staff. In schools where student achievement is improving, a teaching staff is not complacent. They are working individually and in teams to develop new and improved learning experiences for children. Such schools also ensure that teachers have time during the school day to plan together. This need is greater than ever in schools that have adopted the model of including special education students in regular classrooms. Because many professionals, aides, and volunteers will be working in these classes, there must be constant planning to avoid confusion and lost time during the school day.

Along with the need to deal with more special education students in our classrooms, schools must be prepared for an increasing number of minority students, as well as those from varying ethnic backgrounds. An effective school celebrates the diversity of its student body through multicultural educational opportunities. Such projects as Black History Month and model United Nations programs allow students to study racial and national history. On the other hand, a school should guard against creating a society in which each minority group socializes primarily with its own members. One can learn much about a secondary school by visiting the school cafeteria at lunchtime. Are all of the African American students sitting together? Does it appear that those who are dressed in more expensive clothes eat lunch together, while at another table there are kids dressed in black jackets? Our more effective schools work hard to find ways to break down the barriers that separate students. Interscholastic athletic teams, musical groups, and other extracurricular activities often are successful in bringing together a diverse mixture of students.

It is the role of the board of education to observe closely and to analyze all aspects of the school program. This means that board members must take the time to visit school buildings and to talk with students, parents, and employees. Board members cannot effectively monitor the district's schools unless they become "tuned in" to what is really happening. To do this effectively, one cannot rely merely on the reports of their administrators but rather it is necessary to have numerous sources of information. Board members should seek to engage students, parents, and staff in conversations that will help them to see the school from several points of view. Only with this kind of broad understanding can a board member ask the right questions and make the kinds of suggestions that will insure that the schools of the district are truly effective.

NOTES

1. Myra Pollack Sadker and David Miller Sadker, *Teachers, Schools, & Society* (Boston, Mass.: McGraw Hill, 2000), 189.

2. David Clark, Linda Lotto, and Mary McCarthy, "Factors Associated with Success in Urban Elementary Schools," *Phi Delta Kappan* 61, no. 7 (March 1980): 467–470.

3. Samuel C. Certo, *Principles of Modern Management: Functions and Systems*, 3rd. ed. (Dubuque, Iowa: WCB, 1985), 52.

4. Certo, *Principles of Modern Management*, 52.

5. Lowell C. Rose and Alec M. Gallup, "The 30th Annual Gallup Poll of the Public's Attitudes toward the Public Schools," *Phi Delta Kappan* 80, no. 1 (September 1998): 41–56.

6. *Update: Indicators of School Crime and Safety*, 1998 (Washington, D.C.: National Center for Educational Statistics, U.S. Department of Education, October 1998).

7. *Safe Schools, NEA Action Sheet* (Washington, D.C.: NEA, January 1996).

8. Robert Rosenthal and Lenore Jacobson, *Pygmalion in the Classroom* (New York: Holt, Rinehart & Winston, 1968).

9. Judith Azzara, "The Heart of School Leadership," *Educational Leadership* 58, no. 4 (December 2000/January 2001): 62.

CHAPTER 12

Looking Ahead

History has shown that it is presumptuous and perhaps dangerous to try to predict the future. Still, it is increasingly true that, in the words of Gary Marx, "if current systems aren't cutting it, others with an entrepreneurial spirit will be waiting to step in to fill what might become known as an 'opportunity gap.' This is true in education as well as business."[1] There is no question that there are many in this country who feel that public education is not "cutting it." As a result, it would seem that school board members and administrators should become actively engaged in considering ways to change their programs to meet future challenges. In order to do this, we must first attempt to determine how things will be changing in the years ahead.

In his book *Ten Trends: Educating Children for a Profoundly Different Future*, Marx identifies the following trends.

- For the first time in history, the old will outnumber the young.
- The United States will become a nation of minorities.
- Social and intellectual capital will become society's primary economic values.
- Education will shift from a focus on averages to a focus on individuals.
- The Millennial Generation (those born between about 1982 and 2003) will insist on solutions to accumulated problems and injustices.
- Continuous improvement and collaboration will replace quick fixes and defense of the status quo.

- Technology will increase the speed of communication and the pace of advancement or decline.
- Knowledge creation and breakthrough thinking will stir a new era of enlightenment.
- Scientific discoveries and societal realities will force difficult ethical choices.
- Competition will increase as industries and professions intensify their efforts to attract and keep talented people.[2]

Many of these issues have serious implications for public schools. For instance, there is likely to be additional competition from educational maintenance organizations, charter schools, and private and religious schools. There are also a growing number of students who are being educated at home by their parents. Of course, if the voucher program is implemented more widely, it will fundamentally alter our education system in the United States. Even though we cannot know exactly what will happen, a forward-looking community does its best to make its plans based on the best evidence available. Frequently, a board of education will be forced to consider the future in order to make important decisions. This is especially true when deciding whether to close a school, build additions on existing buildings, or perhaps construct new buildings. Without the intelligent study of the demographics, a school district can make serious and costly errors.

In preparing to make a decision involving future building needs, board members need to look at what the national census figures say about their community. Are there any clear population trends in the region and the community? Is the birth rate rising or declining? As much as possible, the board should attempt to gather current and historic information about its own community. A district anticipating a building project or closing buildings should carry out a complete district census. Sending out census forms to all residents is a good beginning, but it is likely only to give a district a representative sample. Even though it is more expensive, it is most effective to send out census takers to visit every residence in the district. A school already knows how many students are currently attending. Administrators will also be aware of the numbers attending private schools or being homeschooled. What will not be known without a census is the number of preschool children who will be entering each year for the next four to five years. Having an accurate accounting of these children, along with the percentage of those who have entered public schools in recent years, is essential to making wise decisions about future needs.

Although these numbers will be helpful, school district officials must also consider several additional factors. What is the current business climate in the district? Is the community likely to lose any large employers? Are there any new businesses planning to come into the district in the near future? Are any of the current businesses considering an increase or decrease in their labor force? This information is most often available from local planning boards or the local chamber of commerce.

Districts also need to look at the national and regional economic outlook. Is the national economy flourishing or experiencing a recession? Could these trends affect the birthrate or the economy in your district?

In addition, a school board must think about the impact of private schools and the trends in home schooling. Is the percentage of eligible children attending local public schools increasing or decreasing? Are there any current plans for the establishment of new private or charter schools? The answers to such questions could affect whether to consider a building project. Even if a district decides that a building project is appropriate, a number of program issues that have to be discussed. For example, should the school have separate computer labs? If so, how many such rooms should be planned? Especially if the project is to build an elementary school, an alternative would be to place enough computers in each classroom that special labs could be omitted from the architectural plan. How many rooms should be set aside for self-contained special education classes? If the district plans to move toward increased inclusion of these students, such rooms might be unnecessary. Still, there could be a need for special education resource rooms, offices for counselors, speech therapists, and also appropriate spaces for occupational and physical therapists. Does the district have half-day or full-day kindergarten? There appears to be significant pressure in many communities to move from half-time kindergarten to full-time kindergarten. If such a change is likely, a district will need to ensure that there are enough appropriate classrooms. With the evidence showing that preschool education can make a positive difference for children who lack advantages in the home, many states and individual school districts are beginning to offer preschool programs in their buildings. A district contemplating such an innovation must plan to ensure that there are classrooms designed for this age group.

The research showing the value of smaller classes, especially at the primary level, has stimulated a national movement towards reducing class size. If this is a likely goal for the district, building plans must provide extra classrooms.

Every district must consider what it will be doing in the area of vocational education. Will there be sufficient enrollment for such courses? With a vast majority of students choosing to go on to college, we need to ask whether school districts should be building large classrooms to teach auto mechanics, cosmetology, and childcare. Are we going to teach an increasing number of advanced placement courses for college-bound students or is the district going to send these students to a nearby college? What about decisions regarding distance learning? Do we need to build specialized rooms to make this type of program available?

All of these and other relevant questions must be considered as a board of education looks to the future. Plans for buildings are only one of the reasons that districts must look ahead. Social trends will also affect our school programs. The future of the American family is a crucial consideration for boards of education as they consider future program needs. In a recent syndicated column, Clarence Page noted that the percentage of out-of-wedlock births in the United States has now reached the alarming rate of 33 percent. For African Americans, the rate is 70 percent.[3] Births by school-age mothers also remain very high. Does this mean that high schools should have day-care centers for the children of their students? Do we need to look more closely at our efforts in the area of sex education? Has the time arrived that public schools should begin to offer required programs in parenting skills? How do we increase involvement of parents when both parents or the single parent are working full-time jobs? This issue becomes increasingly difficult in communities where many parents are working more than one job. Still, we know that school achievement can benefit if we can increase family involvement in education.

Recent research would suggest that influences outside of the school might well have more impact on a student's likely academic success than specific school programs. Even though school officials understand the importance of a child's home environment, it is difficult for a school to affect these conditions. We know that higher family incomes will influence academic results. One explanation that is often given is that more-affluent families can provide better health care for their children. Should some of the money being spent on schools be earmarked for such programs? Richard Rothstein suggests the following societal health initiatives as a way to increase student learning.

- Dietary supplements. In some experimental studies, children given vitamin supplements showed significant test score gains. Vitamin and mineral nutrition supplements are relatively inexpensive.
- Birth weight. There is also an association between very low infant birth weight and poor academic performance. Perhaps a relatively inexpensive investment in the education of low-income pregnant women would lead to higher test scores for their children.
- Smoking. One intervention almost certain to have an impact is reduction of smoking by pregnant women. Smoking by pregnant women has been found to cause an approximate mean decrease of four points in their children's IQ. This would have a big impact on academic test scores. Indeed, the payoff for reducing smoking among low-income women would be great enough that this should be a continued focus of policymakers.
- Lead poisoning. It is widely believed that lead poisoning has been eliminated as a danger to American children, but a nationwide survey conducted recently by the Center for Disease Control concluded that 4.4 percent of U.S. children from one to five years old have harmful levels of lead in their blood. These levels are high enough to affect IQ scores, attention span, reading and learning disabilities, hyperactivity, and other behavior problems. Fewer than 20 percent of children most at risk of lead poisoning in low-income families have been screened for dangerous levels of lead poisoning.[4]

Abuse of drugs and alcohol continues to plague our society. Although the number of students affected by this problem goes up and down, the fact remains that schools are greatly affected by this issue in many ways. Along with the fear of violence, the possible presence of drugs and alcohol in schools has led to prisonlike conditions in many buildings. Students not only have their lockers and book bags searched, there are now specially trained police dogs brought in to find illegal drugs. Ongoing efforts at drug education in schools at best are having only a marginal effect on our students. As we look to the future, our society must do a better job in fighting this problem. Parents, youth organizations, public agencies, and churches, along with the schools, need to come together to collectively attack drug and alcohol abuse. The same is true with our growing concern for violence in the schools. These problems are not going to solve themselves. The use of metal detectors, police officers in the building, and student searches will not end the threat of violence. As communities, we can only make progress with this issue by modeling positive behavior and finding ways to deal with the underlying reasons that children turn to drugs and alcohol and commit violent acts.

As in the past, another major concern of schools will be the ongoing problem of racial integration. Even as we enter the twenty-first century, we are still a long way from ending racial prejudice. A recent report by the Public Education Network and the Education Agenda entitled *Quality Now! Results of National Conversations on Education and Race*

> shows how issues of race continue to influence the performance of students. For example, minority parents shared stories—confirmed by the research—that minority students are more likely than white students to have uncertified or unqualified teachers, dilapidated buildings, and inadequate resources. All of these factors contribute to the persistent achievement gap between white and minority students.[5]

School districts cannot dismiss this problem that continues to be a fact of life in far too many communities. Wendy Puriefoy suggests the following in an article published by *School Board News*:

> First, school boards should welcome a dialogue on education and race. Our community forums revealed that fears about a public dialogue on these issues are misplaced.

While minority parents are cognizant of the role race has played in lowering expectations for their children, these parents are focused not on the past, but on the present—getting the best possible education for their children. Dialogue about education and race can help identify challenges in a way that moves communities from conflict to understanding.

Second, school boards should help provide the public with more and better information. Until parents and community leaders in Hattiesburg, Mississippi, had recently requested it, for instance, state officials had not previously disaggregated test scores or other achievement data by race.

School boards should help ensure that, when possible, test scores and other data are broken down by race so the community can understand the challenges it faces.

Many school board members and school leaders have been reluctant to release such data for fear that it will simply anger or immobilize parents. Our experience suggests otherwise: This information can help empower and engage the public. It can encourage a community to assume a shared sense of responsibility for raising achievement.

Third, school boards should recognize that teacher quality is critical. A recent study showed that in California the poorest communities are eleven times more likely to have uncertified teachers than the wealthiest communities.

This raises concerns about how and where districts assign teachers. School boards have an obligation to see that staffing plans are devised fairly so that teachers without credentials or with a record of poor performance in other schools are not sent packing to poor schools.

Fourth, school boards should encourage outreach to all communities. Race, culture, and socioeconomic class can serve as barriers to minority parents who want to become more closely involved in their children's education.[6]

One way that progress can be made on this issue would be to ensure that there is equality in educational opportunities for all children. Such equality depends in large part on how we finance our schools in the future. The current method for paying for public education maintains a heavy reliance on the local property tax. This method of taxing has created a system that allows communities with high property values to more easily raise the amounts of money necessary to provide quality schools. Despite the fact that there will always be those who will argue that money cannot buy excellence, it is undeniably true that sufficient funds can provide well-maintained and clean buildings, lower class sizes, better qualified teachers, preschool opportunities, and additional educational technology and other instructional supplies.

Even a casual observer who has traveled through our rural, suburban, and urban communities can clearly observe a difference in the buildings and the school campuses. If that same observer could enter the schools, they would be struck by the differences in appearance, supplies, and class size. The differences in educational spending in the United States, and even within the states, are vast. In his book *Savage Inequalities*, Jonathan Kozol

> describes the impact of funding differences through his eyewitness accounts of life in poor schools from East St. Louis to the Bronx. Kozol writes of schools in poor neighborhoods that have no computers and would gladly settle for used typewriters. Schools report a chronic lack of textbooks. Some students go for part, most, or all of the year without a book. Others attend classes so overcrowded that students get desks only when enough other students are absent.

> Despite this nation's wealth, about one in five students attend schools woefully lacking even the most basic facilities. For example, the science labs in East St. Louis schools are forty years out of date. The physics lab has six work areas, each with its own hole where pipes once carried water. The average temperature in the labs is 100 degrees, because the school's heating system tends to roast that side of the building — while the other half of the school freezes. At Morris High School in the South Bronx, the chalkboards are so badly cracked that students are told not to use them for fear they will cut themselves. Plaster and paint chips fall

from the ceiling with such regularity that students shower after school to wash the paint out of their hair. In the band room, chairs are positioned to avoid falling acoustical tiles. When it rains, water cascades down a staircase located just under a hole in the ceiling.

The heart of these savage inequalities, according to Kozol, is the economic gap between poor and rich communities in the United States.[7]

Although in recent years state governments have been increasing their financial contribution to public schools, they have done little to bring about equality in school finance unless forced to do so by the courts. Urban districts have a growing need for additional funds. The unique problems of these schools include the following:

- a higher percentage of students needing special education
- a higher percentage of students needing bilingual or English as a second language instruction
- a higher percentage of children from dysfunctional families
- a higher percentage of students coming from unsafe and unhealthy neighborhoods
- a greater need for preschool programs

These schools need more money to achieve the same educational objectives as suburban and rural schools. There will always be those who will charge that city districts waste much of the money that is given to them by the state. Even though it may be true that some urban districts have been poorly managed and that politics often adversely affects decisions, this is not the fault of the children. As a society, we cannot continue to have close to half of our urban children dropping out of school. Failure to achieve a diploma will continue to endanger a young person's economic independence and will only force our society to spend more on welfare, prisons, and law enforcement.

Property-poor rural districts are facing a similar dilemma to schools in our cities. Even though the educational challenges might not be as great as in urban areas, many poor rural districts cannot compete with the suburbs in recruiting the best teachers or providing the educational opportunities that their children deserve. Individual spending per pupil varies greatly, even within a single state. Wealthy suburban districts might be spending twice as much per pupil than their rural or urban neighbor. Teacher salaries can vary by ten to twenty thousand dollars within the same state.

Why do state governments avoid seeking a remedy to these inequities? While the state-aid formulas in most states will give more aid per pupil to poor districts, nearly every state that has been challenged in the courts has been found to be lax in providing equal educational opportunities. The reason formulas are not achieving this objective seems to be that individual state legislators are primarily concerned about the specific state-aid payments that are made to the schools in their legislative district. Unfortunately, the same is true of most school boards and superintendents. When formulating a budget, a school district has a major interest in what the state-aid formula will do to its budget. School officials judge state legislators based on how well they are advocating for their school districts. With the population shifts in recent years, the political strength of suburban legislators has increased. As urban and rural populations stagnate or decline, state-aid formulas are determined more and more by suburban legislators. The result is that the formulas seem to address the educational inequities within a state in increasingly fewer instances. H. Carl McCall, the comptroller of New York State, recently released an analysis of school aid in New York State for the past four years. During that period, school aid was increased dramatically in the state, but McCall believes that the legislature missed an excellent opportunity to bring about additional fairness in the formula. A study completed by the New York State Council of School Superintendents was quoted in Mr. McCall's report to the legislature. It stated that

> the lack of fundamental change to the categorical nature of most of the recent growth in school aid, and the reliance on a dysfunctional formula driven almost entirely by caps and floors, renders school aid less and less sensitive to differences in school district wealth. As a result, the fundamental policy goal of equalizing educational opportunity . . . is progressively weakened.[8]

If the differences in school financing are great at the state level, they are even more dramatic as we compare one state to another. Given our present method of financing schools, the only way to dramatically affect the difference in educational opportunity and spending from one state to another is for the federal government to play a more active role. Despite the fact that polls during the last decade have consistently shown that education is the primary concern of the American people, the percentage of the cost of public education paid for by the federal government has remained at about 7 percent. No serious effort has been made to decrease the gap in spending between rich and poor districts. In fact, it could be argued that wealthy districts have been in a better position to prepare applications for federal competitive grants. Such districts have been able to hire specialized grant writers while smaller rural districts could not afford such a luxury.

As noted earlier, there is increased support in both parties for a more active federal role in education. At the same time, many members of the Republican Party cling to the belief that increased school choice will help to solve our educational problems. This, along with the party's long-standing commitment to local control of schools, will probably reduce the likelihood of major federal intervention in the effort to provide equal educational opportunity. What, then, can school board members from poorer districts do to help obtain additional educational funding?

To begin with, it is important for rural and urban districts to be active in the annual discussions on the state-aid formulas. State school board associations are an important voice in these discussions, but the leaders of these groups are in a difficult position. They must advocate for all school districts in the state. If they become too outspoken in their lobbying for any one segment of their membership, they will invite internal conflict within their organization. It is also true that the elected leadership of state school board organizations and superintendents' groups are people from suburban districts. Too often, the voices of members from urban and rural districts are silent in the deliberations that create the organizations' legislative programs.

Perhaps a more effective way is to attempt to convince local legislators from poorer districts to become more forceful in their legislative committees and their party caucuses. It is helpful to form alliances with districts that feel they are being shortchanged by their state. In some states, this has meant that rural and urban districts have worked together to affect the legislature. If such a coalition cannot achieve its goals with the legislative branch of their state government, it is possible to sue a state on the grounds that equal educational opportunity is being denied because of the method of financing schools used by the state. Major cases have been won in California, Kentucky, Texas, and New Jersey.[9] In New York State, a lower court decision requiring that the state revise its formula is currently being appealed to the state's highest court.

At this time, it would appear that a legal challenge might be the best way to improve the position of poorer districts. A more permanent solution must lie in a dramatic shift in the way that public schools are financed. The use of local property taxes is not only unfair to communities with a limited tax base but this tax also places a heavy burden on those community members who are on fixed incomes. This is especially true for those whose pensions have no cost-of-living allowances. These senior citizens see the percentage of their incomes being spent on school taxes increase every year. A similar result is likely if schools are financed primarily by a sales tax. If such a method is used, it should not include taxes on items that are essential to the survival of poor people and those on fixed incomes. Unless special amendments are made to the current property tax system, farmers also are forced to pay more than their share. Even though their incomes are low, their farms often are heavily assessed and therefore their tax burdens are extremely high.

Excise taxes on luxury items such as cosmetics, tobacco products, alcohol, expensive automobiles, and jewelry might be a fairer way to raise money for schools. Some states have gone to a state lottery program to help pay for educating their children. Unfortunately, too often those who buy lottery tickets are those who can least afford to gamble. Other states have promoted state-sponsored gambling casinos to raise money for education. Besides the ethical questions that such initiatives raise, neither lotteries nor gambling casinos have resulted in significant increases in revenue from those in our society who are best able to afford increased taxation.

Perhaps the best way to collect money from those best able to pay new taxes is a progressive differentiated income tax. By developing a state income tax without major loopholes for wealthy taxpayers, it is possible to devise a system that results in those with higher incomes paying a larger percentage of their earnings in state taxes. Since the inception of the graduated income tax, this has been the accepted approach, but politically the issue has always been a source of conflict. A number of conservatives in recent years have argued for a flat tax that would use the same percentage figure for all incomes. Although the national Republican Party never adopted this plan, it remains committed to ensuring that no government goes too far with a "soak the rich" tax.

Given these realities, it is difficult to see a rapid solution to the "savage inequalities" that now exist in educational funding in this country. A national priority to seek a system where all children will be able to attend excellent schools is essential. School board members and organizations should be in the forefront of this campaign. One of the areas where inequities show up the most is in the movement to introduce technology into our schools.

As schools look to the future, this is one of the most important issues school board members will face. Currently, there is no question that districts with a high percentage of students from poor homes have fewer opportunities to learn to use computers than students from affluent suburbs. One study has shown that 84 percent of the wealthy suburban schools had Internet access, while only 64 percent of the poorer districts were on-line.[10]

Inequities are equally apparent when we compare the availability of computers at home.

White children are three times more likely to have computers at home than are black or Hispanic children, and they are three times as likely to have computers connected to the Internet. This early computer gap contributes to a later economic gap. African American men between 19 and 54 are the largest groups not using computers. Their salaries average between $11,000 and $20,000.[11]

Although it appears to be closing, there has also been a gap between boys and girls in regard to computer use. Many of the games available on computers emphasize combat and competition, which tend to appeal to males. Studies have shown that boys make up 80 percent of the students in high school advanced computer classes and a similar percentage are computer science majors at the college level. On the other hand, girls dominate the clerical and data entry classes.[12]

Finding ways to deal with these economic, racial, and gender inequities in the use of computers for educational purposes must continue to be a matter of concern for our society. State and federal programs that make additional funds available to poorer communities can be helpful. This assistance can be used not only for hardware and software but must also include significant allotments for training teachers and maintaining the infrastructure. In addition, it is important that the money be available over a long period. Grant money that provides the revenue to start a technology program will run out and the district must be committed to continuing the program even if it is with local funds. Poorer school districts will also have to consider purchasing and maintaining laptop computers for students to use at home. Only if poor children have access at home in the same way that their more affluent fellow students have can we ever come close to reaching technological equality. At least one school district has found a remedy for this problem. The Carmen Arace Middle School in Bloomfield, Connecticut, has made available a laptop computer to virtually every one of its students. Laptops are also available in classrooms, in the library, and even on school buses. The school, which has 90 percent minority students, has provided the following to its students:

1. a rugged notebook computer for every student and teacher; the computers are "childproof," which is almost a necessity in a middle school setting
2. an infrared wireless connection to the school's local area network; no need to plug in the computer—and no danger of tripping over wires—at school or in the home.
3. a low-cost, high-speed Internet connection; students have access to the almost unlimited resources of the World Wide Web
4. ongoing support and professional development[13]

The Carmen Arace Middle School also took the time to develop a complete technology plan. Too many districts have moved into technology without such a plan. In preparing a long-range strategy for technology, districts should take advantage of the technological knowledge of community members, as well as appropriate faculty and staff.

Even with careful planning and a method for insuring equal access for all students, districts must continue to question whether spending large amounts of money on technology is the best way to improve student learning. During the decade of the 1990s, billions of dollars have been spent by all levels of government on technology for schools. Hundreds of communities have passed special bond issues to wire their buildings and purchase hardware and software. Voters have been extremely supportive of such initiatives. Most parents have seen how the computer has altered their own workplace and they wish to assure that their children are well prepared to join the technological revolution. Few doubt that computer skills will be essential for most jobs in the twenty-first century. Perhaps even more important than teaching computer skills (which many students are learning at home) is the fact that the computer is becoming a tool for helping teachers to teach and students to learn. Creative teachers are using the computer for drill and practice, simulation activities, virtual field trips, and personal tutoring exercises. Students are finding it less painful to write compositions because the computer allows them to more easily arrange their thoughts and check their spelling and grammar. Research is much easier using the Internet than spending time with the card catalog in the library. Sources from all over the world can be used while the student is sitting at home or in the classroom.

Individual schools have been seemingly transformed by the use of technology. Teachers and administrators in Willow Bend School in Rolling Meadows, Illinois, claim not only to have created a new level of excitement for learning among their students and teachers but also have improved test scores. In a school where 40 percent of the students are from low-income homes and where a third of the students speak a first language other than English, a major change seems to have taken place. Beginning with the staff development initiative committee, a technology plan was developed. Parents were brought into the discussions at a very early stage. Teachers and administrators attended technology conferences and visited other schools. For three years, the committee worked on a plan to enhance curriculum by implementing new technology.

In spring 1995, Willow Bend ceased to operate as a traditional school. In the following fall, the school doors opened with a new curriculum, instructional approaches, assessment processes, and technology. Students were grouped in multiage settings. Round tables replaced desks because staff understood that learning is largely a social process in which students interact as they explain, support, and self-correct. Folding doors replaced walls to encourage team teaching. . . . Teachers met weekly in teams, and some chose to team teach. Teachers and children formed two K–6 academies to benefit from a small school environment.[14]

As part of a bond issue, all Willow Bend classrooms were supplied with thirty-two-inch monitors and have been wired for video, audio, and data transmission. Classrooms all have at least seven computers, along with additional hardware in the library and resource rooms. Students produce multimedia programs and broadcast videos, which include morning news programs that are broadcast in every classroom. More than forty software programs reside in each student computer. These programs are part of the curriculum in every subject. Visitors come to Willow Bend from schools all over the country to observe the school in operation. As they share their experiences, school officials give the following advice:

- *Change is not neat.* Results do not appear in a linear sequential format. The human spirit is not contained by three- or five-year plans.
- *Leadership is crucial.* Without the principal's enthusiasm, courage, direction, and consistent sense of humor, the Willow Bend experience would not have occurred.
- *Vision directs all efforts.* Willow Bend staff knew their objective from the outset: to create a school enriched with technology that would serve students' learning. All activity was directed toward their accomplishment. For example, teachers placed items about teaching first on faculty meeting agendas. The principal discussed technology use during evaluation conferences. Without that clear direction, we would have lost our way many times.
- *The negative must be minimized.* The "they won't let us," "we don't have the money," "we tried it before and it didn't work," and "there is not enough time" excuses cannot dominate thinking or conversation.

- *Staff must make the decisions.* Although the initial momentum for a technology school came from the central office, local empowerment was a reality. Teachers managed budgets and decided on the purchase of equipment and supplies.
- *Everyone becomes a teacher.* Students taught students and sometimes taught teachers. Parents taught children. One teacher taught another and both learned. Many became experts in different areas and shared their knowledge.
- *Administrative staff was clearly part of the support process.* At Willow Bend, our direction was clearly determined. How to accomplish the task was up to us. The district assisted, provided consultants, and shared our successes.
- *Teachers shared a bias for action.* We planned and acted decisively, did not reexamine every decision, shared clarity of direction, and mustered our courage.[15]

Even though schools such as this are claiming excellent results using technology, many critics claim that an overreliance on computers could actually hinder education. Among their concerns is the fact that they believe that students must develop group interaction skills. Although the workplace has been greatly affected by computers, that same workplace requires employees to work in teams to solve problems. The skills needed to be a leader or even a contributing member of a committee or work group cannot be learned merely by sitting at a computer. Many worry that our students are spending too much of their time in school staring at a computer screen. William F. Roth, in an article entitled "Computers Can Individualize Learning and Raise Group-Interaction Skills," argues that both objectives can be achieved. He believes that the computer can change the primary role of the teacher from an "information giver" to a "learning guide." Roth points out that computers will allow students to better learn at their own rate and that the notion of students moving along one grade level at a time will be forgotten.

Students will be able to keep going once they have mastered a section or topic by simply pushing a button. For example, a sixth-grade student might have a flair for math and be studying algebra, or a third-grader might be completing sixth grade reading assignments, or a second-grader might be pursuing an interest in astronomy.

Because there will no longer be an upper limit in terms of what class members can learn, our traditional evaluation system will lose its meaning. Currently, what is supposed to be learned is defined for a class at the beginning of the semester. Those who come closest to this goal receive the highest grade, usually an "A." The rest of the students define their competitive standing by seeing how close to that "A" they can come.

But because computers allow us to progress at our own rate in each subject, because there is no longer an upper limit to what can be learned, and because the progress of individual students in the different subjects will obviously vary greatly, it will become almost impossible to define an "A." Individual progress will necessarily become the criterion for student evaluation.[16]

In Roth's school of the future, students will be mainly competing against themselves.

At the same times these students are learning at their own rates, group activities should be introduced early in the program. Evaluations should be based, at least in part, on group results, rather than individual test scores. The teacher will become the "facilitator" rather than the "boss" in the classroom. Group assignments will involve high interest projects. In such a classroom, community volunteers will be welcome to assist students, both with their individual and group assignments.[17]

Although there are visionaries who see technology transforming education and even successful programs, such as the one in Willow Bend, the impact of technology on most of our schools has been limited. Still there are some hopeful signs. In 1995, a major program began in the state of Rhode Island.

The Rhode Island Teachers and Technology Initiative has provided laptop computers and sixty hours of training to more than 2,400 teachers — approximately 25 percent of the state's entire teaching force. Besides the long-term goal of improving student performance, the program has three immediate goals, all of which are tied to professional development: to expand the teachers' role in creating their own curriculum; to increase their connection to other teachers and professionals who can be valuable resources; and to improve their personal productivity.[18]

As a result of the plan, observers have noted the following shifts that appear to be occurring.

- from the narrow, restrictive notion of a finite knowledge universe to an expanding knowledge universe rich in context and connections
- from the teacher as holder of all information to the teacher as coach and guide for younger, less-experienced learners
- from repeating the old to creating the new
- from merely gathering information to focusing on essential questions about the information and spending more time on analysis, synthesis, and evaluation
- from valuing only one or two learning modes to drawing on a much fuller spectrum of learning modes
- from learning that takes place primarily through each person's working alone to learning in collaboration with others[19]

Despite the apparent changes occurring in some Rhode Island schools, a final evaluation of the initiative will not be available for many years. In any case, we are still talking about a limited number of teachers in schools who have plunged headlong into the technology revolution. Most school districts have not made this kind of total commitment. Ronald Thorpe summarizes the challenge this way.

> Until massive numbers of teachers decide that the classroom environment must be different in order to do what they most want to do, all other efforts at school reform will amount to no more than what David Tyack and Larry Cuban sardonically have called "tinkering toward Utopia."[20]

While most school districts are jumping on the technology bandwagon, a growing number are calling for moving more slowly. In an article that first appeared in *The School Administrator*, Jane M. Healy argues that "before any more money is wasted, we must pause and ask some pointed questions bypassed in today's climate of competitive technophilia ('My district's hard drives are bigger than yours!')."[21] The author writes of visiting dozens of model schools, where computers are sitting idle and quickly growing obsolete. In some classrooms, the machines were broken and the teachers had not bothered to have them repaired. She mentions visiting computer labs where students quickly finish their assignment and skillfully begin to play "smash and blast" games. Some of her other observations were as follows:

- Many schools had not taken the time to graft technology into their curriculum.
- Too many schools had spent large amounts of money on hardware and software, but had done little to train their teachers to use the equipment.
- A number of technology coordinators had never prepared to be teachers or taught in a classroom.
- In order to finance some technological initiatives, budget cuts had been made in areas such as art, music, and drama.
- Again and again, she saw students wasting time playing games or aimlessly surfing the net.
- There were possible negative physical effects on students who were spending too much time at the computer.
- She also theorized that there might be possible negative effects on the children's brains.[22]

Healy, in an interview published in *Educational Leadership*, talks about the lack of reliable research on the academic impact of computers. The article also raises doubt on some of the studies that have been done. She points out that companies that are heavily involved in educational technology have heavily funded much of the research. Her feelings about this issue are summarized in the following passage.

> The simple fact is that there has been very little objective research done on computer learning. Of that objective research, much of it documents no significant improvement in learning, and some actually shows a decline. Of course, it depends on what we do with the computers. But I have read some very shoddy industry research that school systems have used to rationalize buying huge, expensive learning systems and other kinds of equipment. It's appalling. If you know anything about research, most of this stuff is worthless.[23]

While the debate goes on about the value of computers in schools, board members need to be reminded that there are significant studies showing other proven ways to improve student learning. For instance, there is a growing acceptance that effective preschool experiences can make a significant difference in helping most children. Even with this information, states and school districts have been slow to spend large amounts of money to fund such programs. Although class size reduction initiatives are occurring in some areas, many school districts have chosen to spend their money in new technology rather than hiring new teachers. Such decisions have been made despite the fact that there is growing evidence that lowering class size in grades K–3 will improve student learning. As a result, the critics of the technology revolution suggest that school boards are ignoring proven research in order to be technologically "tuned in."

Others point out the heavy hidden costs that are involved in the introduction and maintenance of computers in schools. Districts must consider that they might have to add new staff, including computer coordinators, computer maintenance personnel, and possibly trainers. An experience of one school district is instructive.

> Roswell, New Mexico, school officials, buying their first computers in 1986, budgeted for incidentals like maintenance and staff training. These incidental costs became much greater than anticipated. With more computers, a growing technology staff had to maintain the equipment and train teachers. Power demands forced an overhaul of the schools' electrical systems. Thousands of yards of wiring were installed to network computers and access the Internet. Costs for everything soared. In the past five years, the 10,500-student district invested at least $3 million on the hidden costs of technology—maintenance and support.

> Quality Education Data, a Denver-based education research firm, says only 37 percent of the average school's technology expenditures go to computers, printers, and similar software.[24]

Often, one-time grants help to begin technology programs; soon after, all the cost must be absorbed by the regular budget. This, along with the ongoing problem of rapid obsolescence of computers is not always considered when a district makes its original commitment to technology.

> In the final analysis, school boards must accept that supporting technology is increasingly costly, experts say. And sometimes those costs won't

be apparent right away. Officials then must make a hard decision on priorities. Says Lee Whitcraft, of Technology and Information Educational Services, a technology cooperative of thirty-eight Minnesota school districts: "So much support needs to go into making a teacher successful in using [technology]. If you're not willing to do that, you should think hard about whether to buy the hardware."[25]

Board of education members in the twenty-first century will be heavily engaged in this ongoing debate regarding the appropriate uses of technology in our schools. There will be voices who might be called the "dreamers," who will talk of the "limitless possibilities for the betterment of learning" offered by technology.[26]

There will be others like Selmer Bringsjord who will talk about the limitations of technology as they point out a machine will never be able to write and produce a play like *Hamlet*. "They don't have feelings: they have inner lives on a par with a rock. No amount of processing speed will ever surmount this obstacle."[27] For this same reason, board members should also be aware that technology will never replace the need for human teachers.

Whatever the limitations for technology, board members in the future will need to make important decisions regarding the use of computers in schools. This issue, along with the others discussed in this chapter, requires that board members make every effort to become well informed prior to committing district resources to costly new programs. This task will be aided by selecting wise and forward-looking administrators. Still, it is true that even with outstanding professional leadership, a board of education will be ultimately responsible for the education of the children of the school district. This heavy responsibility cannot be taken lightly. The pressure of board membership will have an impact on one's personal life and family. Prior to deciding whether to seek membership on a board, the question of the personal implications of board membership must be explored.

NOTES

1. Lawrence Hardy, "What's Ahead for Your Schools," *American School Board Journal* 2000, http://www.asbj.com/evs/00/common.html (7 February 2001).

2. Hardy, "What's Ahead."

3. Clarence Page, "Marriage Going Out of Style, Judging by the Statistics," *Batavia Daily News*, 15 February 2001, 3.

4. Richard Rothstein, "Investing in Family Capital," *American School Board Journal* 2001, http://www.asbj.com/current/coverstory.html (11 February 2001).

5. Wendy D. Puriefoy, "Guest Viewpoint: Education and Race: School Boards Have Critical Roles to Play," *National School Boards Association School Board News*, http://www.nsba.org/sbn/01-feb/020601-7.htm (11 February 2001).

6. Puriefoy, "Guest Viewpoint."

7. Myra Pollack Sadker and David Miller Sadker, *Teachers, Schools, & Society* (Boston, Mass.: McGraw Hill, 2000), 321.

8. New York State Council of School Superintendents study as quoted in comptroller's report "Comptroller Criticizes School Aid," *Councilgram* 3, no. 3 (November 2000): 1.

9. Sadker and Sadker, *Teachers, Schools, & Society*, 321.

10. Pamela Mendels, "Study Shows Disparity in Schools' Internet Access," *New York Times on the Web*, (11 March 1998).

11. Royce T. Hall, "Blacks, Hispanics, Still behind Whites in Level of PC Ownership," *The Wall Street Journal on the Web*, (3 August 1998).

12. American Association of University Women, *Gender Gaps: Where Schools Still Fail Our Children* (Washington, D.C.: American Association of University Women, 1998).

13. Ian Elliot, "A Laptop in Every Backpack," *Teaching K–8* (April 2000): 42.

14. John G. Conyers, Toni Kappel, and Joanne Rooney, "How Technology Can Transform a School," *Educational Leadership* 56, no. 5 (February 1999): 83.

15. Conyers et al., "How Technology," 85.

16. William F. Roth, "Computers Can Individualize Learning AND Raise Group Interaction Skills," *The Education Digest* 65, no. 3 (November 1999): 29–30.

17. Roth, "Computers Can Individualize," 30–31.

18. Ronald Thorpe, "Can Computers Change the System?" *Education Week* 29, no. 8 (20 October 1999): 46.

19. Thorpe, "Can Computers Change," 46, 48.

20. Thorpe, "Can Computers Change," 46.

21. Jane M. Healy, "Why Slow Down the Rush toward School Computers?" *The Education Digest* 65, no. 3 (November 1999): 33.

22. Healy, "Why Slow Down," 34–36.

23. Carol Tell, "The I-Generation—From Toddlers to Teenagers: A Conversation with Jane M. Healy," *Educational Leadership* 58, no. 2 (October 2000): 10.

24. Del Stover, "No Hiding Technology's Hidden Costs," *The Education Digest* 64, no. 9 (May 1999): 36

25. Stover, "No Hiding," 38.

26. Peter C. Scheponik, "A Technology Educator's View from the Trenches," *The Education Digest* 65, no. 4 (December 1999): 61.

27. Selmer Bringsjord, "Just Imagine: What Computers CAN'T Do," *The Education Digest* 66, no. 6 (February 2001): 33.

CHAPTER 13

A Board Member's Personal Life

To this point, we have discussed many current and future issues that will face members of a board of education. Beyond the need to engage in the study and discussion of these issues is the question of how board membership might affect a person's personal life. There is no question that an individual's daily life will be affected by membership on a board of education. As a board member you have become a part of the local government structure and as a result, others will look at you in a new way. Everything about your life will be observed more closely. One group of individuals that will undoubtedly view you differently are the employees of the school district. For school administrators, faculty, and staff, you, and often your family, take on a new importance. As a member of the board that governs the school, you are now in a position to affect the lives of the employees of the district. This is especially true of the superintendent, but it should be expected that anyone who works at the school will see you differently after your election to the board.

If you are a parent with children attending the school district, teachers will become very aware of your children. This can create difficulties for a board member's school-age children. It would be unwise to allow your new status to be a reason for putting additional pressure on your children to work hard and to behave themselves. On the other hand, when the child is old enough, their position as the child of a board member should be the topic of a serious conversation. First and foremost, your spouse and children must understand that they are never to use your status as a board member to try to impress or intimidate employees of the district. A board member's family need not ever talk about the fact that they are related to a member of the school board. If asked about school business, both one's spouse and the children in the family should be advised to say as little as possible.

Family discussions of school matters are inevitable. During these conversations, board members need to be constantly vigilant in order to ensure that they do not discuss confidential issues. Still, it is true that one can learn a lot about the school by listening to family members at the supper table. Even though one should indeed be a good listener, no family member should be given the impression that complaints will lead the district to fire a teacher or principal. The fact is that family members need to be treated in the same way that a board member would deal with other constituents. Private conversations about board business with one's spouse can also be sensitive. Along with the issue of confidentiality, there is the possibility that a couple can disagree on school-related issues. In any case, all family members need to remember who it is that was elected by the voters.

When it comes to dealing with teachers or principals in matters involving the board member's own children, there also must be a separation of the roles of board member and parent. Many teachers are very concerned when they are assigned a board member's child in their class. Administrators do not look forward to disciplining board member's children. If it is possible, the board member's spouse might well represent the couple during parent-teacher conferences or if a parent is called to school on a disciplinary matter. In this regard, it is helpful to have in place a policy that would govern a situation in which a board member's child has a serious discipline problem. In cases where an administrator might normally act as a hearing officer for a student who could possibly be given a long-term suspension, the policy could call for an out-of-district hearing officer. This could save the administrator from possible charges of favoritism or a board member from a community perception that board members' children are given special breaks by the schools administration. Although a board member's spouse might be responsible for discipline problems and individual parent-teacher conferences, the board member should still be active in attending PTA meetings, open house programs, concerts, plays, and sporting events. The most important single consideration for the whole family is to never consider using the position on the board to gain any advantage for the board member's children. Both the spouse and the children of the family must be cautioned about telling a school employee that my mother or father is on the board. If any member of the family flaunts this fact in school, the word will spread very quickly. In too many districts, family members of board members have made veiled threats to school employees. Any such action, even by younger children, undermines not only the moral authority of that member but also that of the entire board of education.

Another inappropriate action by a board member is to attempt to give direct orders to school employees. An individual board member has no authorized power to be a hands-on manager in a school. This is the responsibility of the school administrator. Collectively, the board does make policy, but implementing and enforcing these regulations is the job of the school administration. If students are misbehaving at a school event, a board member should report the problem to the staff member in charge. When board members perceive there is a problem in a specific building, the normal procedure would be to contact the superintendent. It would then be the chief school officer's job to work with the building principal. In some districts, the superintendent is not uncomfortable with the board member going directly to the appropriate administrative staff member. This procedural question should be carefully discussed with the superintendent when a new board member takes office. For some superintendents, it is disconcerting when a board member works directly with a middle-level administrator. Allowing the superintendent to deal with all of the potential problems will also save time for the board member.

Time is a problem for most people who serve on boards of education. Although when one decides to run for a position on the board it may appear that it will only be one or two meetings per month, it will soon become evident that the obligations go beyond the regular meetings. This is especially true with those districts that function with board committees. A significant committee structure can more than double the amount of time spent at meetings. In addition, board members will need to set aside time to study the written information provided before each regular meeting. There may also be times when one is asked to participate as a speaker or as part of a panel at school or community events. Participation in formal occasions, such as an honor society induction or graduation, may also be considered part of a board member's duties. This is especially true for the board president.

There will be times when members of the board wish to demonstrate their concern for school employees. If an administrator who works directly with the board has a death of a family member, a board member should consider paying his or her respects. Such gestures demonstrate a personal support and concern for school employees. The same is true for board members who attend retirement dinners and staff recognition programs.

Of course, there will always be the phone calls from constituents requiring that a board member investigate potential problems. Sometimes such calls will come during the dinner hour or at other inconvenient times. Whatever the timing of the call, it is essential that the board member or an administrator promptly follow up on the issue and make a return call to the concerned constituent.

People who seek election to boards of education are often active in other community organizations. Many are involved in such programs as Little League or other sports programs. They also could be active in civic groups, such as the Rotary Club or the Kiwanis Club. Others have obligations to their church or synagogue. Because of these many commitments, it is not unusual for board members to be away from home three to five nights a week. Such a schedule can detract from one's family obligations and leave a spouse to become the primary parent. Because of this danger, it is advisable for board members to evaluate carefully their other commitments. It may well be necessary to reduce one's obligations to other groups when becoming a board member.

One should also consider the need to maintain a healthy lifestyle. It is important that time be left for regular exercise and that community obligations do not cause board members to neglect their health in other ways. Most of all, board members should not sacrifice their families in order to become "an organization power" in their community.

Another consideration is the impact of board membership on one's full-time occupation. At one time, many employers actively encouraged their employees to seek community leadership positions. Although some companies still urge their employees to be active participants in civic activities, others are neutral on the subject. Because of the current trends toward downsizing, many employees are working longer hours than ever and as a result both evening meetings and release time during the day have become a problem for a number of potential board members. In any case, it is probably advisable to discuss potential board membership with one's employer prior to making the decision to become a candidate.

Not only can your participation on a board of education affect your employer, it can and does alter your position in the community. Board members are like other elected officials in that their fellow citizens, as well as the media, will carefully observe them. A board member who is arrested for drunken driving can expect that the problem will be prominently reported in the press. Such a story might well be headlined "Board of Education Member Charged with DWI." Both you and your immediate family will be the subject of community discussion if you have any type of public problem. A board member who is seen publicly intoxicated or acting in a rowdy manner at a sporting event will be the subject of gossip in many communities. Unfortunately, your family will also be subjected to the same public scrutiny. If a board member's children are in trouble, it will be talked about both in and out of the school. Especially in small communities, a board member must expect that their personal life will be less private. This is a price one must pay for holding elected office in a democracy. As a community leader, you should always seek to be a model for others. For some, this responsibility is disturbing, but it can also be seen as a challenge. By being someone who others can look up to, a board member is providing a public service to their community.

The responsibilities of board membership must be taken seriously. To do the job well, board members must establish priorities in their lives and then develop plans to ensure reasonable schedules. The obvious factors to be considered would be, first and foremost, one's obligation to family, religious responsibilities, a person's primary occupation, exercise and other leisure activities, as well as other community responsibilities. It is important to develop a weekly and monthly schedule that can include all of these items. Your work on the board must take a high priority in this schedule. Doing so will necessitate that board members may have to exclude themselves from other community functions during their tenure on the board. We have now reached the point where the reader who is considering membership on a board of education can attempt to arrive at a personal decision. This will be the subject of the final chapter.

CHAPTER 14

Making the Decision

Having considered many of the important issues facing school board members, as well as the impact of board membership on one's personal life, it is now possible to turn to the primary question raised by this book. The reader must now face the very personal decision of whether to seek a position on their local school board. In attempting to answer this question, a potential board member should attempt to answer the following questions.

1. Am I willing to give the necessary time to study the issues and to participate in the many meetings and other events required of board members?
2. Am I willing to consider giving up some other community and personal interests to assure that I have sufficient time and energy to meet my new responsibilities?
3. Am I, and is my family, willing to accept the additional scrutiny from the community that is caused by board membership?
4. Am I able to take on this position without adversely affecting my family obligations?
5. Am I going to help or hinder my primary career by accepting a position on the board of education?
6. Am I prepared to speak before small and large groups and spend a considerable amount of time in meetings?
7. Am I able to deal with stressful situations that occur during serious debates over important public questions?
8. Am I able to sleep at night when facing complicated and unresolved dilemmas?

9. Am I able to compromise and live sometimes with ambiguity?
10. Am I able to make a decision and not cause myself anguish by constantly second-guessing myself?
11. Am I able to admit my mistakes and possibly take the heat when things go wrong?

In deciding whether to seek board membership, a potential candidate must weigh the answers to above questions and ask whether the potential problems identified are enough to discourage further consideration of the matter. If one feels comfortable at this stage, there are still several more difficult questions to ponder. These questions all have to do with the possible motives that are causing a person to seek board membership. It is important to think about the following questions:

1. Am I really vitally interested in the issues that will face me as a board member?
2. Am I considering this because of single issues, such as the need to reduce taxes or the desire to fire the superintendent?
3. Am I a person with the necessary skills and knowledge to make a positive contribution to the board?
4. Am I seeking board membership primarily to add a community service component to my rèsumè or as a "stepping stone" to higher office?
5. Am I really deeply concerned about the education of the students in the district?
6. Am I willing to accept the criticism that I will inevitably receive as a board member?

In regard to this final question, it is important to know that those involved in education will constantly be the target of educational critics. Those who complain about our public schools have the attention of the public. A best-selling book by Martin L. Gross, *The Conspiracy of Ignorance*, speaks harshly of the failure of American public schools. On the cover of the paperback edition there is a quote from a review that appeared in *The Atlantic Monthly* that boldly charges "that our school system had fallen into the hands of people with small ambitions and second rate brains."[1] In the same book, the author states unequivocally that "elected school boards have abdicated their powers to the hired help, the Education Establishment."[2]

The criticism of national detractors will have far less impact on local board members than what they are likely to hear from their friends and neighbors. When the school district signs a contract with any of its employee groups, there will be those in the community who will complain about the salaries being paid. This will be especially true of teachers and administrators. Board members will be reminded constantly that their professional staff works only ten months each year. Although this is untrue, especially for administrators, school board members can expect to be on the defensive in most communities when discussing salaries. Complaints about individual teachers and specific programs will be frequent. Various groups in the community will be seeking additional funding for their favorite programs. While frequently encountering lobbyists and critics, there will be very few occasions when board members will receive any kind of expression of gratitude for their service. Members of the administration they regularly work with will hopefully create occasions to recognize those members who have faithfully served as board members. It is always good to at least have a "thank you" dinner for someone who is leaving the board. In any case, one cannot expect to receive frequent public praise from the community.

The rewards of the position are more personal. There is no question that a board of education can make a difference when they are able to create a positive environment for students and district employees. It is this potential to do good things for people that creates the greatest satisfaction for board members. There is also the opportunity to watch the success of the employees who have been hired by the board and to witness policies and programs that have been adopted improve the school district. Finally, it can be a very positive experience working with other people on real issues. Many lifelong friendships have evolved between people who have worked together on a board of education.

Perhaps the greatest source of comfort for those who choose to serve is the knowledge that what they are doing is important to their community. Aristotle said, "All who have meditated on the art of governing mankind have been convinced that the fate of empires depends on the education of youth. Educated men are as much superior to uneducated men as the living are to the dead."[3] Few would disagree with the proposition that the education of young people is the responsibility of any society that will be most important in determining the destiny of that nation. As an elected member of a board of education in the United States, the stakes are very high. Alexis de Tocqueville observed in his book, *Democracy in America*, that "the health of a democratic society may be measured by the quality of functions performed by private citizens."[4] In the United States, we are in great need of committed and talented people who will take on the important role of board of education membership. The future of our schools and our country will in large part depend on the decisions made by these people.

NOTES

1. Martin L. Gross, *The Conspiracy of Ignorance* (New York: Harper Collins), cover.

2. Gross, *Conspiracy of Ignorance*, 15.

3. George Seldes, compiler, *The Great Quotations* (New York: Lyle Stuart), 304.

4. Seldes, *Great Quotations*, 274.

Index

About the Author

Bill Hayes has been a high school social studies teacher, department chairman, assistant principal, and high school principal. From 1973 to 1994, he served as superintendent of schools for the Byron-Bergen Central School District, located eighteen miles west of Rochester, New York. During his career, he was an active member of the New York State Council of School Superintendents and is the author of a council publication entitled *The Superintendency: Thoughts for New Superintendents*, which is used to prepare new superintendents in New York State. Mr. Hayes has also written a number of articles for various educational journals. Since his retirement in 1994, he has chaired the Teacher Education Division at Roberts Wesleyan College in Rochester, New York. He is the author of *Real Life Case Studies for Teachers* and *Real Life Case Studies for Administrators*, published by Scarecrow Press in 2000, and *So You Want to Be a Superintendent?* published in 2001.